My Comrades and Me

Staff Sergeant Al Brown's WWII Memoirs

Al Brown

Copyright © 2011 by Al Brown.

Library of Congress Control Number: 2011900759
ISBN: Hardcover 978-1-4568-5396-9
Softcover 978-1-4568-5395-2
Ebook 978-1-4568-5397-6

All rights reserved. No part of this book may be reproduced or transmitted in any form or by any means, electronic or mechanical, including photocopying, recording, or by any information storage and retrieval system, without permission in writing from the copyright owner.

Photo credits to Bill Mauldin's WWII cartoons

This book was printed in the United States of America.

Copyright TX 5-923-055
February 2, 2004

To order additional copies of this book, contact:
Xlibris Corporation
1-888-795-4274
www.Xlibris.com
Orders@Xlibris.com

Al's identification tags (Dogtags)

Contents

Acknowledgement and Appreciation 11
Foreword 17
Infantrymen 19
Memoirs—Motive and Motivation 20
My Rewards 24
Shell Holes and Bomb Craters 28
The Dogface Soldier 34

MY BASIC TRAINING PERIOD

Wheeet! Wheeaa! 43
6X6X6 45
Do Something, Even if it's Wrong 50

ANZIO BEACHHEAD EXPERIENCES

A Long, Lonely Night 55
Pete Deanda 59
My First Day 65
My First Foxhole 71
A Darby's Ranger, Almost 76
Koppelschloss 79
Anzio Shep 83
Ringside Seat 85
Beachhead Spies 87
Party Line 89

Paintbrushes, Stencils, and Blue and White Paint 91
Anzio Annie 93
Get Off the Beach 97
ALTEO 100
One Tiger, Three Shermans 102
A Tragic Night 105
My Encounter with a Flare 107
Pfc. Myles F. Pratico 110
Sacrificial Lambs 113
Walla from Walla Walla 116
A Very Bad Night 119
A Foxhole View of the Air War 123
Brothers Meet, Head to Head 127
Two Beady Eyes 133
A Very Special Memory 135
My Worst Day 137
My Brother 142
First Lieutenant Eric W. Tatlock 144
Negligent, Lost, and Lucky 150
A Lost Day 155
A Plan Not Needed 158
The Failure at Anzio 160

SOUTHERN FRANCE

First Extraction 167
Purple Onion 172
Very Dull Day 176
D-Day, Southern France 177
Stop it Yourself 189
An Angry Shell in Flight 192
A Sergeant's Revenge 195

Saved by a Chapel 198
Romberger's Close Call 203
Saved by a Chapel—Epilogue 207
My Confession 214
Second Reunion 218
Oops! 223

COLMAR POCKET

Colmar Pocket, the Other Bulge 229
The Night before Christmas, 1944.....................................234
Rude Awakening 237
The Other Murphy 239
A Dash in the Snow 243
Clark's Helmet 251

GERMANY WEST OF THE RHINE

Lucette Libert..257
A Close Call in Rimschweiler 261
Stupidity at Rimschweiler 264
Beer in Zweibrucken 267

GERMANY AND AUSTRIA

Bad Decision Leads to Mini Bridgehead across Rhine 271
Anxious Moments in a Barn...276
Nurnberg Medic 278
Final Thoughts and Memories 283
False Alarm 286
Why Not Me?..288
Nein Heil..289

SPECIAL COMRADES

General Lucian K. Truscott..293
Iron Mike..295
Lieutenant Pergament 299
Lt. James Alfred Pringle 303

MY TWO CENTS

Defenseless America 309
Glory...312
My Enemy Was Not My Enemy..315
The Niceties of War...317
The Truth about the US WWII Bazooka.......................................321

PUP TENT POETS

Foreword...329
Hatred's Yield 331
Hey Bud 332
Order 334
Dirty Gertie*..335
Fanny Of Trapani 336
Luscious Lena..337
Marie Of Napoli 338
A N Z I O 339
Air Raid 341
I Hunt Today..342
The Rangers*2 343
Conversation With A Mule...346
The Mule Replies...348

Photo Gallery...349

Dedication

These memoirs are dedicated in honor and in memory of the WWII rifle companies whom we supported with our machine guns.

Rifle companies drew the most horrific lot imaginable. They met the enemy eyeball-to-eyeball and cleared the way for all other units. The casualty rate among rifle companies was the highest of any other military units. Following close behind these men, I witnessed unimaginable horror and heroism. Just the short distance between us and the riflemen made a big difference in survival. God bless them all.

Acknowledgement and Appreciation

Several years ago I was fortunate in making the acquaintance of Denis Toomey. Denis has created the most wonderful website (dogfacesoldiers.org). It is built around a gallery of photos and information on WWII. Also included are veterans' memoirs as well as a photo gallery of veterans, and many other features. It is a web site to explore.

The featured photo gallery is a collection of photos created by the Photo Section of the Third Infantry Division's Reconnaissance Platoon. This section was comprised of five men: Edward W. Cole, William Heller, William J. Toomey, Robert S. Seesock, and Howard B. Nickelson. Denis is the son of William J. Toomey.

Denis has generously dedicated his website to the advancement of information about WWII. He is especially generous with space for WWII veterans and their families.

It is with his generous approval that the author is able to share a number of photos from the dogfacesoldiers.org web site, and for which I am forever grateful.

Images from this site will be identified by the notation (courtesy dogfacesoldiers.org).

Top: Third Infantry Division Insignia (Worn on left sleeve just below the shoulder)

Bottom: Thirtieth Infantry Regiment Insignia (Worn on both lapels and hat)

Insignia Thirtieth Infantry Regiment

Coat of Arms Thirtieth Infantry Regiment

Symbolism:

The rock, inscription, and wyvern refer to the two designations by which men of the 3d Infantry Division are popularly known, i.e., "Marne Men" and "Blue and White Devils."

The "Rock" represents the division's firm stand against the German offensive at the Marne River in World War I. It was there that the commanding officer, Major General Joseph Dickman, stated "Nous Resterons LA" (we remain here), when asked by the French Army Commander how soon the Third Division would follow his order and begin withdrawing.

The wyvern, an heraldic form of the devil, bears the division's blue and white stripes on its wing in commemoration of the division's action at Anzio, Italy, in World War II where they were called "Blue and White Devils" by the enemy.

Battle-weary soldiers of the Third Infantry Division eagerly swallow a hot meal near Bult, France after having been relieved from seemingly endless days of combat in the Vosges.

Borrowed with respect from The History of the Third Infantry Division in World War II

Foreword

WWII Experiences

We veterans, after returning from the war, wanted only to put the war behind us. We had no interest in reliving it. Besides, who wanted to hear of the horrors of war? The entire country had seen and heard enough of it.

So, we found jobs, went to college, got married, started families and in general got our lives restarted.

The years go by fast when you are going to work every day and spending weekends with wife and children. Before you know it, the children are all grown up and have started families of their own.

Now that we veterans of WWII are getting into our twilight years, we find that people seem to be showing a genuine interest in our stories. In every issue of "The Watch on the Rhine", my Division's newspaper, are printed letters from relatives of the men who served in the Division. They are all seeking information about their fathers, uncles and grandfathers who have died without sharing their military lives and experiences with them.

I have tried to help these people when I can. In a few cases I have known the person for whom information was sought. In those cases I have been able to be very helpful. In other cases I have been able to find some helpful information from the two histories I possess. One is the history of my regiment in WWII and the other is the history of my division in WWII.

The letters from these people tell me that, someday, one of my children or grandchildren may want to know about my war experiences and me. With that as a possibility, I have decided to put some of my experiences in writing while I am still able to do so. Recent prodding, and much support from my wife and other family members, is no less of an incentive.

I have tried to be selective in my choices of stories. I have no desire to dwell too much on the daily gore of combat. I have tried to select experiences that I think have some interesting point to them. I have tried to also mix in a bit of humor here and there.

I want to especially thank my darling wife and best friend, Jo Ann. She not only encouraged me to write these stories. She was my very diligent proofreader. Many errors are missing from these pages because of her sharp eye.

Al

Infantrymen

By

Edward M. McGuire

I saw them just this morning
As a hundred times before
Forever walking, dragging,
I wonder if they know what for.
Mechanical beings they seemed to be,
Like men from another world.
With nothing but loneliness and death:
Wages for hours toiled.

Edward McGuire was a tanker in Cannon Company, 7th Infantry Regiment, 3rd Infantry Division. Edward wrote the above poem while sitting on his tank one morning watching the infantry moving forward into combat. This poem was published in The Stars and Stripes Mediterranean newspaper.

Memoirs—Motive and Motivation

The memoirs in this book are not the result of a decision to write a book. These memoirs are the result of evolution over a period of twenty-plus years.

After my retirement in 1985, I began responding to letters in *The Watch on the Rhine*, the bimonthly news publication of the Society of the Third Infantry Division. The letters were from veterans' families seeking information about their husbands, fathers, brothers, uncles, and grandfathers who had passed on without sharing their experiences.

Following are portions of a few of the letters from *The Watch* and from other letters addressed to me personally. Personal information has been excluded:

> *My father, J—O—, received a Silver Star as a Private in company E of the 15th Infantry. Do you know of any way that I could learn more about his actions? He never discussed them prior to his death.*

> *My husband's father was an infantryman in the 30th Infantry Regiment, 3rd Infantry Division during WW II. He was killed in France on Dec. 2, 1944. We believe it happened during*

the last several days of the Vosges Campaign(?). He is buried in the Lorranine Cemetery in St. Avold, France. Would you have known—?

I was wondering if you would have any information on my uncle. His name is—.

I'll tell you what I know. He fought with the 7th Infantry Regiment, 3rd Infantry Division. He was KIA on 1-23-1945.

Dear Mr. Brown,
This is a note to say a huge thank you for writing your memoirs. For some time now I have wanted to know more about my Dad's time in the army during WWII but only had bits and pieces of things he had told us and which my Mom also recounts. He was in the 7th infantry 3rd division but beyond that I do not know which company etc.

My name is L—B— and I am looking for any connection to my uncle, Sergeant F—B—. My uncle was with Co. B, 1st Bn. 30th Inf. Regt., 3rd Div. He was killed on December 17, 1944. I believe he was in the area of Kaysersberg, France when he died.

I am really enjoying reading your memoirs of WWII. My father, E—C—B— of C—, MS, was in the 3rd Division, Company F of the 30th Infantry. He rarely talked about the war—he said he had spent all his life trying to forget it. He died almost 20 years ago from cancer and I wish I had asked more questions.

From my own experiences, along with my copies of the 3ID and 30IR histories, I was able to provide information to these people.

From the division roster section, I could determine a soldier's rank and the company, battalion, and regiment he was in.

From the roster, I could also determine if the soldier was KIA, MIA, or POW.

From the military awards section, I could determine any medals that the individual had earned.

From the dates that he was with the division, I could determine the battles that the individual's unit had participated in, and I would provide his family with the details of these battles. In some instances I had known the soldier personally, and in those cases, I was able to provide a great deal of detailed information.

After ten-plus years of providing information to other veterans' loved ones, I began to think of my own situation. I was no different than the veterans whose families I was helping. I had not shared my experiences with my family. I decided to do something about it.

In the year 2000, I wrote my first memoir, the one titled *My First Day*. It was my plan to write my memoirs and leave them in my computer for the family to discover after my demise. Since then, the number of memoirs has grown to what is in this book.

In 2005, a friend asked permission to put my stories on his web site, dogfacesoldiers.org. I agreed, and as a result, I began getting requests for information from veterans' family members who had read my stories. This greatly increased the research that I was doing for veterans' families and, at the same time, made me realize that my stories were not just "my stories" but my comrades' stories as well. We had these experiences together, so why wouldn't they be our stories? At that point I began to write with the idea that I was writing for them as much as for myself. This gave me an increased incentive to continue.

If, from reading the stories contained in this book, the families and descendants of WWII infantry soldiers are able to find answers to their questions about their soldier's combat experiences, I will be amply rewarded.

My Rewards

I mentioned that, over the past twenty-plus years, I have done what I could to provide information about WWII soldiers' combat experiences to their loved ones. I have been amply rewarded for my efforts as you can see from the following portions of letters that I have received from them. It is these warm expressions of appreciation that, in addition to being rewarding, they create in me the desire to continue.

Brownie,
You are awesome man!!!! My wife brought home the mail today and in it was the book you prepared just for me! I appreciate that more than words can tell.

Dear Mr. Brown,
This is a note to say a huge thank you for writing your memoirs. For some time now I have wanted to know more about my Dad's time in the army during WWII but only had bits and pieces of things he had told us and which my Mom also recounts.

Dear Al,
Morris just returned from the post office (we have to go to the post office for mail in our little town) and had more information from you. I will admit he brought it home about an hour ago and I became so interested I forgot about everything else so noon lunch was late!

How can I ever thank you or repay you for all you have done to help me know of my brothers last days of life?

Dear Mr. Brown,
How can I ever thank you for what you have put together? Yes, it was a perfect ending to Memorial Day, 2010. My dad would not talk a lot about the war—only a few times when I expressed interest and pushed a little harder to get information out of him.

Hi Al,
I picked up the binder from my parents house today, and I am extremely happy. It's beautifully put together. The maps are amazing, and knowing about the battles is very helpful. It is my new prized possession.

Dear Al,
I received your package today, and I was so excited about the photos and the articles. I have never seen the pictures of Dad in Anzio. I will send Dad and Audrey a copy of the photos; I know they will appreciate it. Dad is in fairly good health but his memory is almost gone.

I really appreciated the story that you told about Dad. I have never heard that one before. You definitely have not disappointed me; you have been most helpful! Thank you again for all of your help.

Dear Al,
I do not think I have taken the time to just say a Big thank you for your help. Not only for helping people like myself today, but what you sacrificed, and went through so many years ago. Take care my friend.

Hi Al,
Thank you so much for the information that you sent me. It was very informative.

Graphic showing organization of the Third Division.

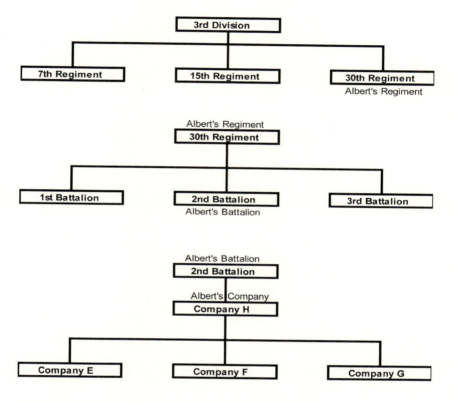

This graphic is to help visualize the makeup of the 3rd Division and how Albert's Company H related to all the other units.

This graph only deals with the infantry units which are the primary combat units. However, there are a number of support units that add greatly to the division's overall fighting force. These units, and the number of them, will vary according to strategic needs for specific operations. They will include, but not be limited to, four to six artillery battalions, reconnaissance platoon, quartermaster battalion, signal company, tank units, engineer battalions, medical units, etc.

Shell Holes and Bomb Craters

There are three types of holes made by bombs, rockets, mortar shells, and artillery shells.

Type I Hole: No hole

Now, "no hole" sounds like a very good thing, but really it is not. No-holers are the worst kind because they produce a much wider dispersion of shrapnel. No-holers are normally produced in three ways. One way is by fuses set to explode a certain height above ground. Another way is when, in a forest, the shells strike tree limbs and explode prior to reaching the ground. No-holers also occur in rocky, mountainous terrain. Shells exploding on rocks do not make holes, but they do produce a maximum of shrapnel in all directions. This type is especially vicious because one cannot dig a hole in rocky terrain. All three no-holer types should be avoided whenever possible. All are equally effective on the target.

Type II Hole: Small narrow hole

These are the best kind and are most favored by those on the receiving end. They are produced by what is termed "a dud." While these are the most favored, it is also very wise to move away from one as fast as possible. You never know when a dud will change its mind.

Type III Hole: Relatively large bowl-shaped hole

These are made by bombs, rockets, mortar shells, and artillery shells that strike the ground and do what they are supposed to do, explode.

The diameter and depth of these holes vary substantially. There are many factors that affect the diameter and depth of type III holes. The most common factors are the following:

1) Size of the projectile.
2) Angle of approach.
3) Condition of the ground that it lands in. Soft, wet ground permits deeper penetration prior to exploding, thus creating a deeper and wider hole than if it lands on hard ground. Ground can be naturally hard or it can be frozen.
4) Type of fuse. The fuse can be timed for ignition at impact, or it can be set for a brief delay. Delayed fuses are used when trying to penetrate buildings, bunkers, or armored vehicles. When these shells miss the intended target and strike the ground, they make a deeper and larger hole than the so-called "point detonation" shells do.

Generally speaking, the larger and deeper the hole, the better the recipient likes it. Deeper penetration results in more shrapnel being absorbed into the ground. Deeper penetration also results in shrapnel flying more upward than outward.

The marks of artillery on the Anzio beachhead is seen surrounding The Factory. By the time the German's had regained this landmark in mid-February, more than 100,000 Allied troops populated the beachhead although this number was eclipsed by the German troops they faced. The Allies were holding their lines yet, still ahead, was a massive German offensive that would strike at the end of February.
(aerial photograph by Jack Cole and courtesy dogfacesoldiers.org)

The hospital area at Anzio was a busy place handling over 18,000 combat wounded out of 29,200 total Allied casualties for the Anzio action (the German casualties are listed at 27,500). The hospital area was not immune to artillery and air attack and was hit several times during the beachhead stay. The medical units on Anzio suffered 89 killed and 387 wounded.
(aerial photograph by Jack Cole)

The Third Division HQ was established at Conca in a group of buildings known as "The Castle". Although the beachhead forces faced little resistance at the time of the landings, by mid-February Field Marshal Kesselring had mustered ten divisions under his 14th Army to face the beachhead. His orders, direct from Hitler was to drive the enemy "abscess south of Rome" back to the sea.
(aerial photograph by Jack Cole)

The town of Aprilia housed what was known as "The Factory". Located in the British Sector of the beachhead, The Factory was captured in late January but a German counterattack in early February put this strategic observation point back in their control for the rest of the beachhead stay.
(aerial photograph by Jack Cole)

The Dogface Soldier

"The Dogface Soldier" was the exclusive song of the Third Infantry Division during WWII. After the war, other units heard the song and just naturally gravitated toward it. They also made some modifications to the words.

This was our marching song that was always played with great enthusiasm by the Third Division Band at every parade we had. It inspired us like no other marching song. The band would begin "Dogface Soldier" just before the front ranks passed in front of the reviewing stand. The instant the strains of "Dogface Soldier" swept across the parade ground, a change would come over the entire regiment, and ordinary marching became sharp and inspiring to everyone who participated and observed.

Our band never passed up an opportunity to play it for us. The most appreciated and moving times were when we would be moving forward for a major assault. Our band would be there beside the road playing "Dogface Soldier" until we were out of earshot.

I was told by the men who came over with the Third for the invasion of North Africa in November, 1942, that the words were written by a soldier aboard ship. The soldier already knew the music (I do not know who the composer was) and he put the words to the tune and entertained the troops aboard ship by singing and playing it on his guitar. The song made an instant hit with the men, and shortly after the landings, the Third Division Band picked it up and began playing it. Shortly after that, it became the official Third Division Song.

To this day it is still the Third Division's official song. We sing it at all our reunions and other gatherings.

THE DOGFACE SOLDIER

Moderato

I would-n't give a bean to be a fan-cy pants mar-ine — I'd ra-ther be a dog-face sol-dier like I am —: I would-n't trade my old O D's for all the Na-vy's dun-ga-rees for I'm the walk-ing pride of Un-cle Sam —; on all the post-ers that I read it says the Ar-my builds men — so they're tear-ing me down to build me o-ver a-gain — I'm just a dog-face sol-dier with a ri-fle on my shoul-der and I eat a kraut for break-fast ev'-ry day —. So feed me am-mun-i-tion, keep me in the Third Div-i-sion, your dog-face sol-dier boy's O — kay.

WAR

You wish to see?

Take my hand.

Walk with me.

Browning Water Cooled Machinegun WWI & WWII.
In WWII it was referred to as Heavy Water Cooled Machinegun.

The gun with full jacket of water weighed 47 pounds.
The tripod weighed 51 pounds.
Water can, full, weighed 20 pounds.
Full (250 rounds) canister of ammo weighed 20 pounds.

Note: The ammo feed is from left to right. This picture can be confusing to someone not familiar with the gun. The belt portion containing ammo hanging from the right side of the gun is not normal. Normally, when loading, the metal extension is passed though the receiver from the left without raising the breach cover, which is hinged, and the gun will begin firing from the first round in the belt. In this picture, it is obvious that the breach cover was opened and the belt of ammo was placed with thirteen round to the right of the breach. This caused the gun to begin by firing the fourteenth round from the end. (Image copied from a Google web site.)

My Basic Training Period

Wheeet! Wheeaa!

I had been in the army about two weeks when the following events occurred. I, like a few million others, was a civilian one day and a serviceman the next.

I was in the army but had not yet made a full transition to soldier. I was referred to as "soldier" but was not yet a soldier. That came later.

On this day, I and another "soldier" were on garbage detail. A corporal, who drove the truck, was in charge of the detail. We would pull up to the garbage rack outside each mess hall in the regiment. The cans were loaded onto the truck with all of their contents. When the truck was full, the cans were taken to the camp dump and emptied.

We had just stopped at this mess hall next to one of the camp's main roadways. I had jumped out of the truck to hand cans up to the other private who stayed in the truck, when I heard a large number of marching feet. I turned my back to the garbage cans to see what was going on. Well, I saw at least forty WACs (Women's Army Corps) marching four abreast (no hidden message intended) marching toward where I was. They were being led by a lady colonel who counted cadence occasionally to keep them in step.

They were all officers of every rank from second lieutenant to major. They were dressed in cotton olive drab fatigues. Around their waists was a regulation army cartridge belt which supported a canteen of water on their hip. The cartridge belt gathered their uniforms in at the waist, thus accentuating their already hourglass figures. I, being a guy, found this to be very pleasant to watch.

Now, in those days it was quite common for guys to whistle approval of a cute chick. It was considered a way of paying a compliment. Well, with me being still more civilian than soldier, I could not resist. As the marchers were almost in front of me, I let out one of my very best Wheeet! Wheeaa! whistles. I watched the ladies a few more seconds and then turned to pick up one of the garbage cans. When I turned, I came up against a body in my path. My eyes were about level with the middle of his chest. I looked almost straight up and saw a very angry one-star general looking down at me. I suddenly felt two feet shorter than I already was. I took one step back and attempted a very awkward salute, which the general ignored. He asked, "Private, who is in charge of this detail?" I replied, "The corporal in the truck, sir!"

The general turned toward the cab of the truck and ordered, "Corporal, stand down, now!" The corporal sailed out of the truck and saluted the general. Without acknowledging the salute, the general gave that poor corporal the chewing out of his life. He told the corporal that if he could not maintain proper discipline over the men under his command, he would pull his stripes and pass them on to someone who could.

The corporal took his chewing like a man and never took it out on me. I just wanted to crawl away and hide.

6X6X6

I entered the army March 12, 1943, at Camp Blanding, Florida. I and my brother, Frank, were sworn in together and then sent to Fort Jackson, South Carolina, for basic infantry training. We were assigned to the 106th Infantry Division. I was in the 422nd Infantry Regiment and Frank in the 424th.

Prior to Pearl Harbor, our army had been reduced to a mere token of a fighting force. Too many of our citizens would not lend support to a strong defense. After all, we had two oceans protecting us. Ha!

According to *www.history.army.mil/documents/wwii/ ww2mob.htm*, actual active army strength, April 1940, was 230,000, and actual army strength on December 31, 1942, was 5,397,674 with a goal of 8,800,000.

Because of the great and sudden need for combat troops, existing divisions were not in sufficient number, and several new divisions were commissioned. The 106th was one of those divisions. Because there were so few trained soldiers, regular army soldiers were reassigned to other divisions throughout the country to act as a nucleus training cadre. As a result, about 90 percent of the training cadre was made up of new inductees. The ones who enlisted earlier were selected to train those who followed. The greatest deficit was in trained commissioned officers. It was a sort of blind-leading-blind scenario.

I write the foregoing to provide an understanding of the setting and situation under which the following experience occurred. One can easily see that there could be a professionalism deficit under such circumstances. I will add that by the time basic training was completed, we looked and acted like real soldiers.

The following took place toward the end of the first month of basic training. The division's commanding general decided that the enlisted men were far too negligent in showing proper respect to commissioned officers, i.e., there was not enough saluting going on to make him happy. His solution was to detail "saluting police" to catch and report infractions. Of course, these "saluting police" were junior commissioned officers (first and second lieutenants). Since most infractions took place during off-duty hours, the officers had to perform these duties during their otherwise free time. Complicating matters more, the officers were assigned a quota that they had to meet each day before they could be free to do other things more enjoyable.

Well, we enlisted men were aware of the general's campaign and were doubly motivated not to be caught. One, we did not want the punishment that followed being reported. Two, we did not mind if the officers were up past midnight trying to meet their quotas. It was not long before the officers began working in teams to set traps for us.

One Sunday afternoon I was returning from visiting my brother in his barrack. I was passing through a little park area that had several shade trees and benches scattered about. As I was approaching one of these benches located about twenty feet to the right of the sidewalk I was on, I noticed a soldier sitting on the end of the bench, but not in the normal fashion. He was turned at ninety degrees to the normal sitting position, and with his back toward me. Well, I was immediately alerted that this might be an officer but could not be certain at first. As I got closer, I saw that it was an officer, so I intended to salute him as soon as I was in a position that he could see me and could acknowledge the salute. I kept my eyes on him constantly hoping that he would turn my way, but he did not. I waited until I was just a little past him so that he could not help but see me. I then turned in his direction and rendered the required courtesy, which he reluctantly acknowledged.

I then turned to continue on my way, and after two or three paces, I heard a loud "Soldier!" from behind me. I turned around to see another lieutenant stepping out from behind a tree that had been on my left. While I was distracted by the officer on the bench, I had bypassed the one behind the tree without saluting him. I did salute him after he stopped me, but it was too late.

He already had his pad and pencil out and was demanding my name and the company that I was from. I protested the entrapment, but to no avail. I was reported, and the following Sunday afternoon, my first sergeant ordered me to dig a 6X6X6 behind the company supply building. (A 6X6X6 is a hole six feet square and six feet deep. By the way, I was a towering 5'3" at the time.)

The general's campaign did little to promote respect for our officers. We understood their plight and had some sympathy toward them. All sympathy vanished when they began to cheat. We did respect the rank and the responsibility that went with the rank, but not the man.

The sergeant had already marked off the 6'X6' square in which I was to dig, so with shovel in hand, I began. After an hour or so I had dug about half of my six-foot depth requirement when my shovel hit something metallic. I got down on my knees and dug around the object with my hands. It turned out to be a real live fragmentation hand grenade, not a training grenade.

I took the grenade to the company orderly room to show the first sergeant, thinking that he would allow me to dig in another location. Instead, he ordered me to continue digging. He wanted to know what else might be there. I pleaded with him to let me fill in the hole, and I would gladly begin another 6X6X6 at another location, donating the work I had already done. I did not win. He ordered me to continue the excavation and to pile everything I found outside the hole.

Within the next two feet of digging, I found enough ordnance to overfill a large wheelbarrow. I found another fifteen or twenty hand grenades, a number of bazooka rockets and mortar shells, plus several canisters of machine gun and rifle ammunition. Of course, that two feet of excavation was done largely by hand, and very slowly.

Also, as the hole got deeper, the berm of excavated dirt got higher and steeper, the dirt would slide back into the hole as I threw it out with my shovel. To overcome this, I had to climb out of the hole occasionally and move the berm farther back from the hole. By the time I was about four feet deep, I had difficulty climbing out of the hole. I found an empty wooden crate in the back of the supply room that I dropped in the hole to serve as an exit platform.

The sergeant had provided lanterns for me to see by, and the hole was finally completed about 9:00 p.m., having worked nonstop and without the evening meal. After the sergeant checked the depth to see that it was 6', I handed up the wooden crate that I had been using to get in and out of the hole and the sergeant kindly helped me out. He then tossed a cigarette butt into the hole and ordered me to bury it. There is an army regulation somewhere that prohibits work details as punishment. The detail must have some legitimate purpose. Burying the cigarette butt was his justification for having the hole dug.

It was nearly midnight when the backfilling was completed and I could go to my barrack, hungry and exhausted, where I slept like a rock until 5:45 a.m., when we were awakened with the usual lights on accompanied by the sergeant's loud whistle to begin another week of training.

To my knowledge, they never determined when or why the explosives were buried there. My guess was that there had been a supply sergeant involved in some shady dealings in military hardware and had to bury the evidence prior to an audit.

Do Something, Even if it's Wrong

In our basic infantry training it was constantly drilled into us that we should "do something, even if it's wrong." This rule applied no matter what the situation or circumstance. The rule was intended to emphasize that it was better to do the wrong thing than to do nothing. Doing nothing when confronted by the enemy was the worst thing possible. Even doing the wrong thing might turn out to be the best thing, because the enemy would not be expecting it.

This episode is about the time that an officer seized upon a golden opportunity to demonstrate this point to us.

We were in the hand grenade throwing phase of our training. We had been drilled in the proper way to throw grenades, but using dummy grenades. Now we were at the hand grenade range for our first experience in throwing real, live grenades.

They were running one squad at a time through the training procedure. There were a total of twelve men in a rifle squad. So, for safety, there were thirteen foxholes previously prepared for participants to jump into after the grenades were thrown. Twelve holes were in a line, one for each man in the squad. One hole for the range officer was located to the right of the enlisted men's line of holes. It was also a few feet in front of the enlisted men's line of holes so that he could observe each man to see if he was using the "proper" technique and "form." Under the procedure, all twelve grenades would be thrown simultaneously.

The procedure required four specific commands from the range officer. They were the following:

1. **"Stand."** At this command, every soldier was to take up his throwing stance that called for both hands to be in front of the thrower and below his waist. The grenade must be in the throwing hand with the safety lever against the palm. (If the fingers hold the safety lever, it could be accidentally released prematurely if the thrower relaxed his grip on the grenade.) The ring that is attached to the safety pin must be well in the grasp of the index finger of the non-throwing hand.
2. **"Pull pin."** At this command, the soldier simply pulled the safety pin and remained motionless with both hands still below the waist while the range officer checked each man to determine that his pin had been properly pulled and that the soldier was still maintaining proper form.
3. **"Prepare to throw."** At this command, the soldier must bring his throwing arm up and behind him in the proper manner. The non-throwing arm must be extended horizontally and pointing at the intended target and with the fingers also extended. The soldier must hold this pose while the range officer checked each man for proper form and technique.
4. **"Throw."** At this command, the soldiers finally get to throw their grenades simultaneously and jump into their foxholes for protection. At this point, the range officer also jumps into the hole prepared for him.

When my squad was having its turn at demonstrating its throwing skill, we only got as far as the **"Pull pin"** command. After pulling the pin on his grenade, one of the soldiers lost confidence in the safety provided by the safety lever. He promptly threw his grenade. When the grenade is thrown, or released, the safety lever flies off, permitting the firing mechanism to strike a percussion cap, which, in turn, ignites the fuse. At this point the grenade will explode in five seconds.

When the percussion cap is struck, it makes the same sound as a cap pistol. Hearing the cap pistol crack of the other soldier's grenade, the rest of us immediately threw our grenades and leapt into our holes without awaiting further orders from the range officer. The first grenade exploded, and two seconds later, eleven more exploded almost as one.

When I and the other soldiers raised our heads above the ground, there stood the range officer outside his hole. He had not moved. Not expecting what happened, he was caught off guard and had done nothing. By some miracle he had not been hit by one of the fragments from the twelve grenades.

I saw this incident as an excellent example of the "Do something, even if it's wrong" rule. The eleven soldiers, who threw the grenades after hearing the firing cap of the first grenade, did what was wrong under the range procedures but were much safer than the officer who did nothing.

Anzio Beachhead Experiences

A Long, Lonely Night

As stated in other stories of my WWII experiences, I joined the Third Division in Italy on Thanksgiving Day 1943.

The division had just been relieved from the frontline and was bivouacked in an area surrounded by a number of artillery batteries that maintained a fairly constant hammering of German positions. This was the nearest that I had been to frontline positions so far.

The next day, I was called for guard duty. There were a dozen or so guard posts in and around the encampment. One was along a ridge overlooking our camp. The ridge was probably five hundred feet above the camp and was about two hundred yards long. It also lay between our camp and the enemy.

The army has very specific orders pertaining to one's responsibilities while on guard duty. They are in two categories: "General Orders" and "Special Orders." General Orders apply to all posts regardless of location or circumstances. Special Orders apply to a specific post and are special because of that post's location and/or special purpose.

The Special Orders for the post overlooking the camp were as follows:

1. To walk the length of the ridge from end to end, back and forth, continuously.
2. To be on constant alert for enemy patrols that might try to penetrate our perimeter.
3. To watch the sky for possible enemy paratroop drops.
4. To alert the camp of a possible air attack.
5. If any enemy activity was observed, fire three rifle shots to warn the camp below.
6. If there was an enemy ground attack, that post was to be abandoned after giving the appropriate warning, and the duty soldier assigned to that post was on his own to join his unit below.

As you have probably assumed by now, that is the post that I was assigned to. Duty shifts were for four hours. From 6:00 p.m. to 10:00 p.m., 10:00 p.m. to 2:00 a.m., and 2:00 a.m. to 6:00 a.m. I drew the 6:00 p.m. to 10:00 p.m. shift.

Each guard detail is composed of a number of soldiers equal to the number of guard posts to be manned, plus a corporal. The corporal is known as "the corporal of the guard." When one shift of guards is relieving another, both corporals accompany the shift going on duty. The corporal going off duty goes along so that he can be assured that all of his men get properly relieved.

The trail that led up to the post that I was to guard was very steep and slippery. The old corporal of the guard stayed at the bottom of the trail with the other men in my shift, while the new corporal of the guard and I made the climb to relieve the man then on duty. It was still light as we made the trip up, but it would soon be dark. I was not real happy with the post that I had drawn but was determined to make the most of it.

It had been raining a slow, steady rain for several days and did not show any sign of letting up. Most of the soil in Italy is heavy clay that turns to mud when wet. It is also very slippery. It was very difficult to walk the length of the ridge without losing my footing several times with each trip across.

As I alternately walked and fell, my mind was constantly on my Special Orders for this post. I was especially concerned about number 6. I listened for sounds of possible infiltrators. I watched the sky for paratroopers. For me, every sound was an enemy. Our artillery was booming around me, their flashes lighting the area for brief instants. Often, in one of these flashes, I would think I saw the silhouette of an enemy soldier.

This went on for seemingly endless hours. After I decided that my four hours had passed, I began pausing for a few minutes at the end of the ridge from which my relief was to come, in hopes that I would hear them coming. When no relief came, I began telling myself that in my impatience for relief, I was letting my mind run in double time. I told myself that if I did not think about the passage of time, it would go faster.

This went on and on until I was absolutely convinced that my time was up, but still no relief. Finally, the sky to the east began to lighten up. This was my confirmation that I had been left to serve three shifts. As 6:00 a.m. and full daylight arrived, I heard voices coming up the trail.

When I met my corporal, who waited at the bottom of the hill, I asked him why I had not been relieved. His lame, unacceptable excuse was that he had forgotten that I was up there. I think I knew why he did not come. My first thoughts were to report him to the officer of the day, but after having breakfast and more time to think about it, I decided to let it pass. The upside was that the corporal was not from my platoon and that I would not be going into battle under him. Besides, I only wanted to sleep and put the longest, loneliest night of my life behind me.

This is not the end of the story. About 9:30 a.m., this corporal awakened me from a sound sleep and ordered me to get dressed. I was going on guard duty again. This time it was going to be the battalion commander's tent. I could see me at my court-martial for falling asleep while guarding my battalion commander. I respectfully declined the corporal's kind offer. I told him that I was not fit for guard duty and that it would be irresponsible of him to give me the assignment.

At this, the corporal raised his voice and informed me that he was giving me a direct order to get up and to go on duty. If I did not do so immediately, he would report me to the officer of the day. I said, "Great idea. Report me to the OD."

He reported me, and before I could fall asleep again, the OD was outside my tent ordering me to come out. I came out immediately and gave the OD my very best salute. He asked why I was refusing the corporal's orders to go on guard duty. I told the officer that it was because I was unfit for guard duty. I then explained to him that I had just come off the guard post on the ridge after three continuous shifts because I had not been relieved. He asked the corporal if that was true. The corporal acknowledged that it was. The OD ordered me back to sleep and left with the corporal.

I learned later that the corporal had pulled that shift guarding the colonel's tent.

Also, the next day in the chow line, I noticed the ex-corporal was no longer wearing his stripes.

Pete Deanda

I often think of Pfc. Peter G. Deanda, or simply Pete Deanda, as he was known by the troops.

As I have stated in reports of other events, I came to the Third Division Thanksgiving Day 1943. The division had just been pulled from the front. We did not know it at the time, but the Third Division was selected to spearhead an assault landing near Anzio. The landing took place on January 22, 1944. In the meantime, the division went through very intensive training for the mission. The training included several practice landings from various landing craft.

That two-month period was valuable to me in that it allowed me to learn a lot about combat from the men who had been there. It also gave me the opportunity to really get to know Pete Deanda.

I noticed that Pete was a loner and without close friends in the company. It wasn't that he was reclusive or standoffish. Actually, I thought that he was very outgoing and friendly. But for some reason, the men who knew him longer than I merely responded to him in a friendly way. No one seemed to claim him as a close friend.

He came over with the division and participated in the landings in North Africa and all battles in Africa, Sicily, and Italy up to this time. He had always performed exceptionally well in combat, and all that knew him had great respect for him. Yet he did not seem to have a best friend. It made no sense to me.

I had only been with the division a week or two when Pete began to cultivate my friendship. I guess it was my small one-hundred-thirty-pound frame and baby face that made me nonthreatening to him.

Pete was from Tyler, Texas, and immensely proud of it. He idolized the famous Texan. One of his favorite things was to challenge newcomers to guess whom Tyler, Texas, was named after.

I soon learned that he was illiterate. He would have me read his letters from his girlfriend back in Tyler. He would dictate letters to me to send to her.

Pete was from an Apache father and a Mexican mother. He was very handsome. About six feet tall and perfectly proportioned physically. He had hair that would change from jet black to a very dark auburn, depending on how the light would strike it. He was very proud and always perfectly groomed. He and his uniform were always ready for inspection. He was a very good and disciplined soldier.

All of the above statements about his amicable demeanor and character were true. But as I learned later, only when he was sober. I say in his defense that he was sober most of the time. He would only drink when away from camp on leave, or was AWOL.

During this two-month training period, passes were few and far between. About midway in the two-month training period, some of us were granted passes to visit Naples. Pete was one of the lucky ones, or unlucky ones, depending on your point of view.

Pete returned from his night in Naples well past curfew and escorted by two MPs. As a matter of fact, we had already had our daily, before-breakfast, five-mile speed march. We had finished breakfast and were on "police detail" when Pete was brought in. (Police detail is where the soldiers form a line across the company's camp area and walk along picking up every piece of litter, no matter how small.) The first sergeant had Pete join in on police detail.

It was then I met the other Pete Deanda. I then understood why it was against the law in Texas to sell alcoholic beverages to the Indians.

Pete was mean and surly. He kept trying to pick a fight with anyone and everyone. He screamed for everyone to shut up whenever anyone spoke. Then, when everyone kept quiet, he shouted at us for being too quiet. I was stunned at his behavior. But I understood why the other men never got close to him.

The only way to deal with him was to stay out of his way until he sobered up. Once he was sober, the amicable Pete returned. He would apologize to everyone for his behavior. And he would cry big tears. He cried because he was ashamed of his weakness. He once told me that a good brave did not lose control of himself and that his father would be very unhappy with him.

Pete and I continued in our close relationship. I found a lot of good in him. Also, he was a good man to have on your side in combat.

Our preparation for the Anzio invasion continued. Pete stayed out of trouble until January 20, 1944. He went AWOL after the evening meal. When we were rudely awakened about 3:00 a.m., January 21, to stand muster, Pete was not there.

At this 3:00 a.m. muster, we were instructed to prepare our packs for combat, strike tents, leave our duffel bags at a specified point for pickup by our quartermaster, and be ready for breakfast at 4:00 a.m. We were to load on trucks at 5:00 a.m. for transportation to an unspecified destination. From our special training, we knew we would soon be aboard a ship. We just didn't know its destination.

When Pete was reported AWOL, Captain Greene, our company commander at the time, announced to all assembled that, if Private First Class Deanda missed this upcoming event, he would spend his next twenty years in prison doing hard labor. We all knew that he meant every word.

Our platoon leader asked me to prepare Pete's combat pack and to get his duffel bag of personal belongings to the pickup point. He then persuaded the company commander to leave me behind to watch for Pete. I had to come with the cooks on one of their jeeps with or without Pete. The cooks would be last to leave because of the time it would take them to pack up all the stoves and other cooking paraphernalia.

I was happy that Pete was going to be given a chance. I gladly put his pack together and gathered all his personal belongings into his duffel bag and dragged his and my bag to the pickup point. I got his mess kit out and filled it with the morning's bill of fare, snapped the lid on tightly, and hoped that he would show in time to eat it.

Trucks arrived on schedule. Everyone except the cooks and me loaded onto the trucks; and shortly after 5:00 a.m., Company H, Thirtieth Infantry, moved out for the docks at Naples harbor.

I kept my eyes on the ridge that Pete would be coming over if he returned. I guess a half an hour went by, but no Pete. I could see by the progress they were making that the cooks would be ready to leave within another ten or fifteen minutes.

About that time, in the gray light of dawn, I saw Pete coming over the ridge. I ran to meet him. He was drunk.

He looked at where the camp had been and asked what was happening. I told him that he was going to prison if he didn't shape up.

I told him the deal. I helped him with his pack and rifle. We got in the back of one of the jeeps where Pete made a stab at eating breakfast as we bounced along toward Naples harbor.

When we arrived at the dock, I helped Pete from the jeep, and we headed for the area where I had been told Company H would assemble. In another ten minutes, Pete and I were back with our company.

Naples harbor was a busy place. There were more ships anchored in the harbor than I could count. Every foot of docking space was being utilized by a variety of ships. Everyone had his orders and deadlines to meet. Troops and vehicles were all vying for maneuvering space on the dock. Troops had to be loaded of course. But the supplies that they were going to need also had to be loaded.

As we were pushing our way toward the LST that we were to board, a truck was inching along very slowly. The driver was being very careful not to endanger the troops that practically surrounded his truck. I saw Pete, still wobbly on his feet, very close to the truck's left front fender. Pete moved a little sideways and encountered the truck. Pete was in his usual mood when drunk. He blamed the driver for crowding him. In a burst of anger, Pete opened the driver's door, pulled him from the truck, and began punching him hard with both fists.

Several men, more his size than I, moved in to stop Pete. It took about four men to hold him. A first lieutenant that was nearby moved in and ordered the men to restrain Pete until the MPs could take over. With that, Pete freed his right arm and flattened the lieutenant on the spot.

When the MPs arrived, Captain Greene instructed them to put Pete aboard the LST to be dealt with later.

Finally, after we were all loaded, I wanted to check on Pete. I found him in his bunk crying so loud that everyone in the compartment could hear. Huge tears flowed down his face. He wanted me to help him find the officer that he had punched so that he could apologize.

After Pete was fairly sober, he was summoned before the company commander. Captain Greene told him that he was going to give him one last chance. But if he messed up again, he would be court-martialed and that Captain Greene would charge him with every past breach of discipline on his record. The charge of striking an officer would be a very serious charge. He would be dishonorably discharged and would definitely be in for some prison time.

Well, Pete made the landing and participated in the beachhead fighting for about three months until one night, Pete and a shell fragment met. His wound was severe enough to end his career as a soldier.

After release from the hospital, he was honorably discharged and returned to Tyler, Texas.

Pete Deanda's wound was a blessing. It saved him from disgrace and prison. It would have been impossible for him to not foul up again.

My First Day

A few minutes before two on a dark moonless morning, January 22, 1944, many assault boats moved at full throttle toward a beach near Anzio, Italy. The sea was very calm. I was in one of those assault boats. Not only was this to be my first assault landing, it was to be my first day in combat.

I was the number 3 gunner in a water-cooled machine gun squad. My combat load consisted of a canister of water for cooling the gun and a canister of ammunition for the gun. Other members of the squad carried two canisters of ammo each for the machine gun. The canister of water and the canister of ammunition weighed twenty pounds each. In addition to this forty-pound combat load, I also carried a nine-pound rifle with ammunition for it, entrenching tool, combat pack with blanket, shelter half, extra clothing, personal items, rations for three days, and a gas mask. My total load had to be eighty pounds or more. My body weight at the time was one hundred thirty pounds, and my height was five feet four inches. You could say that I was not dressed for swimming.

We were in LCVPs (Landing Craft Vehicles and Personnel). These craft carried up to forty men. The craft I was in hit a sandbar about one hundred yards from shore. We were all thrown forward as the craft stopped abruptly. Being in the front, I was slammed hard against the forward bulkhead that was also a ramp when dropped and was a reluctant cushion for the men behind me.

An LCVP is rectangular in shape and sits very deep in the water when fully loaded, as it now was. Because of this rectangular shape and deep draft, it creates a very large following sea, or wave. As this following wave passed under our craft, it lifted us off the sandbar. Our coxswain was prepared for this lift and immediately gunned the engine to full throttle. The boat lunged forward twenty or thirty feet, but not enough to clear the sandbar. Our craft was now stuck with its stern on the sandbar and its bow over deeper water. The coxswain made several full throttle efforts to move forward, but it was useless, the boat was stuck fast. The coxswain dropped the bow ramp and ordered everyone out.

When the ramp dropped, the entire front of the boat was open to the sea. A huge wave rushed in, and in one or two seconds the water was above our knees.

As mentioned, my position was in the very front and on the port side. As I stepped off the ramp, I was completely submerged. My helmet was lifted off my head as I went under and, as I learned later, flipped over and floated away. I know this because my squad leader found it when he went back into the sea looking for me.

By tiptoeing, I was just barely able to keep my mouth above water but had almost no traction for forward progress. The taller men behind me were crowding me in their haste to get ashore, making it difficult for me to maintain my balance. I turned to my left to let them pass, and in so doing, I stepped into a hole that put the water about two feet above my head.

There I was, in deep water and weighed down with a heavy combat load. It never entered my mind to drop the ammunition and can of water. The can of water is especially important to the machine gun. The gun cannot fire long without water for cooling. Besides, I still would not have been able to swim if I had released the ammo and water cans. I knew that I was in big trouble at this point, and that panic was now my enemy. I must not panic!

Without hesitation, I dropped into a crouch and leapt up and forward as hard as I could. The momentum of my jump carried me to the surface for a quick breath before being sent to the bottom again, where I crouched and leapt to the surface for another quick breath. I repeated this procedure again and again, still clinging to all my equipment, including the water and ammunition canisters. With each leap, I made a little progress toward shore.

I finally reached a depth where I could keep my mouth above the surface. I just stood there on my tiptoes filling my lungs with much-needed air and thinking how fortunate I was that the water was very calm that morning. Had there been waves of any consequence, I doubt that I would have made it.

After a minute or two, I regained enough strength to work my way into shallower water and finally wade ashore. As I drew near to where the other men from my squad were waiting on the beach in the darkness, I heard my squad leader, Cpl. James Pringle, telling them that he had found my helmet floating upside down near where I went under but that he had not found me. Then I heard Pfc. Leonard Troutman, number 1 gunner, exclaim, "Oh my god, he had the water can!" In response to Troutman's concern for my good health, I wanted to announce my arrival by dropping the water can on his foot.

I did forgive Troutman. His concern for water to keep his gun operative was well founded. He and all the men were overjoyed that "Brownie" had not drowned as expected.

I had been the only man not present when the squad checked off on the beach. Corporal Pringle went back into the sea to look for me. That is when he found my helmet. He told me that he had even felt for me with his feet.

Now that everyone was accounted for, we moved out to a predetermined assembly area where our section leader, Sergeant Marcantel, reported to the commander of the company we were to support that day. We were ordered to follow close behind the riflemen and to be ready if needed.

The riflemen moved out with First Section, First Platoon, Company H, following closely behind. Thus began my first day of combat.

Daylight found us, still wet from our dunking in the Mediterranean, moving cautiously through a forest. Sergeant Marcantel, armed with a carbine, was walking in a crouch like an Indian stalking his game. Sergeant Walla, squad leader of the second squad, said, "Hey, Marcantel, what are you going to do if a bunch of Krauts jump up in front of you?" Marcantel replied, "I'll empty this carbine into the lot of them."

Before I give Walla's reply, you need to know that the carbine was fed ammunition via a clip that was inserted from the underside of the carbine. The clip held fifteen rounds. On the right side, just in front of the trigger guard, were two buttons. One was the safety release. The other was the clip release. Press the clip release button and the clip will drop out.

Walla replied, "How many do you think you will get with one shot?" At that, Marcantel, and all that were in on the exchange between them, took a good look at his carbine. There was no clip in it. The clip of ammo was still back at the assembly area where we began. Intending to take his weapon off safe, Marcantel had pressed the wrong button and ejected the clip.

To compound matters further, the carbine was still on safe and would not have fired anyway. Sergeant Marcantel took the ribbing that followed in good spirit. This broke a lot of tension as we continued forward. It helped me a great deal. I learned that you could take humor into battle if you chose to.

By midmorning we were moving through an open field. The sun had dried our clothing completely. I was carrying the machine gun at the time. It was common practice for us to exchange loads with the number 1 and 2 men to give their shoulders a rest. Number 1 carried the tripod. Number 2 carried the machine gun. I was number 3, as stated earlier, and had traded with number 2 to give him a break.

Suddenly, there was shooting ahead of us. The call went out for the machine guns to come forward. Corporal Pringle and Private First Class Troutman dashed forward to a shallow ditch where Pringle wanted the gun set up. I followed close behind with the gun. Troutman set the tripod where he wanted it, and I placed the gun on the tripod and moved to one side so that the number 2 gunner could take over and assist with the firing of the gun.

To my surprise the number 2 gunner had hit the ground when the shots rang out and had not moved. The rest of the squad behind him had followed suit. They were all flat on the ground. I called to soldier X (I choose not to use his name) to bring the water can and ammo forward. But he was frozen and could not move. I ran back and took the water and ammo from him and told the others to get their ammo up to the gun position. I returned to the gun and helped Troutman prepare the gun for firing.

We never knew what the shooting was about. We were never given a target to fire on and in a couple of minutes were up and moving again. Corporal Pringle changed my assignment to number 2 gunner and moved soldier X to last position in the squad. Soldier X was transferred to Battalion Headquarters Company the next day. So before noon of my first day, I had moved up one position in the squad.

In fairness to soldier X, I must report that he overcame whatever it was that caused his inaction that morning. He later volunteered for the Battalion Battle Patrol and served honorably to the end of the war.

My First Foxhole

Note: Foxholes are not for foxes. They are for soldiers. That's just what they are called.

January 22, 1944, we landed on the shore of the Mediterranean Sea near Anzio, Italy, at 2:00 a.m. (See "My First Day.") The Germans were caught by surprise, and the landings were almost unopposed. We met very minor resistance as we moved inland. We knew that the Germans would be sending opposition forces as rapidly as possible. But not knowing the enemy's capabilities or timetable, we were prepared for contact at any moment. We spent the entire day moving cautiously forward until, by nightfall, we were five or six miles from the beach where we had landed.

Soon after dark, we were ordered to dig in and establish defensive positions. Leonard Troutman and I began to search for a good location for our machine gun. Troutman had arrived from the States just a few days ahead of me. This was going to be our first foxhole under combat conditions.

We noticed a concrete wall about two feet high that was well enough in line with the other defensive positions being established. We decided that the wall would be a good protective palisade to fight from if we were attacked.

The wall should stop small-arms fire with no problem, and the machine gun could easily be set up high enough to fire over the wall. It seemed like a winner, so we began to dig our hole as close to the wall as practical.

We had barely begun when we became aware of an unpleasant odor. There was a masonry outhouse about ten feet from our hole, but that was not what we smelled. Investigating in the dark, we discovered that the wall we were digging behind was one of two walls at the edges of a concrete slab about fifteen feet square. The walls met at one of the corners of the slab. Stored on the slab, and against the two walls, was animal manure.

With this discovery, we considered digging in another location. But the anticipated protection from small-arms fire outweighed having to put up with the odor. Anyway, we figured that we would get adjusted to the smell after a while. So we stayed with our first choice and continued digging.

The ground was very hard, and digging was difficult. We would break loose an inch or two at a time with our pick and then remove the loose material with our shovel. After an hour or more we were only about a foot deep. But the real problem was that water was beginning to seep into the hole. Water would splash on us every time the pick struck the ground. But so what, if it rained we would be wetter than from the splashes. Besides, there was the protection from small-arms fire to be considered. So we continued digging.

The water made digging more difficult. The clay soil that we were digging in became very plastic and gooey after we hit the layer where the water began. The wet clay would stick to the pick, and we had to pull it off with our hands. Progress became even slower. But that was OK. Once the hole was completed, we would have protection from small-arms fire. Also, we would have our own private john with the outhouse only ten feet away. So we kept digging and bailing water.

Finally, after about two hours, we were barely two feet deep, and water was coming in even faster. We decided that because of the water, we would not be able to make this a hole that we could stand up in. But that was OK. We would just lengthen it to what the army calls a slit trench that we could lie down in. We would be below ground for protection from artillery and mortar shell fragments, and we still had the wall for protection from small-arms fire. So we kept digging and bailing.

It must have been about two the next morning when we decided to call it quits. The hole was long enough, and we both agreed, grudgingly, that it was deep enough. Besides, we didn't have enough energy left to dig another grain.

January nights in Italy can be very cold. We discovered this once we stopped the vigorous exercise of digging. We bailed the water from the hole, wrapped ourselves in our blankets, and settled in for what was left of the night. We both fell asleep almost immediately.

At the crack of dawn we were jarred awake by a bang as loud as a thunderclap. My first thought was that one of our tanks must be close to our hole and had fired at something. I looked around. There was no tank in sight. I saw other guys from our platoon with their heads up looking around as puzzled as I was.

Then it happened again. This time I knew what it was. A German Tiger tank was firing at a road intersection about five hundred yards behind us. Our "private" john was directly in line with his target. The shell passed no more than a foot above the outhouse. I happened to be looking in that direction when the shell passed. I saw the red tile shingles jump in its wake.

When a high-velocity shell passes that close, it makes the same sharp crack that the gun makes. It's as though the cannon is right there, not several hundred yards away.

The firing continued for at least half an hour. It fired one shell every minute or two. But this was not our only concern. While we had slept, the hole had filled with water. Our blankets and clothing were completely soaked with foul-smelling water. We were also shivering in the cold morning air.

We wanted to get out of the hole to bail it out and to wring the water from our blankets but did not feel safe getting out of the hole with 88mm shells shaking the outhouse every minute or two. So we just lay there, speculating as to what would happen if the Tiger lowered its aim by a foot and hit the outhouse. We concluded that we would get a lot of concrete chunks along with shell fragments in our hole if that should happen.

I then began to wonder what would happen if the Tiger's crew spotted our positions and put a few rounds in the manure pile. Or even worse, what if a shell struck our little two-foot wall? I figured we would get even more concrete and shell fragments than if the outhouse were hit.

Finally, after ten minutes had gone by without a shot being fired, Troutman and I decided to get out of the hole. First we bailed the water out. Then we wrung out our blankets. All this was done while lying down, because we were afraid that we would be seen if we rose higher than the wall. Next, we stripped and rolled up in our blankets while we wrung out our clothes. After putting our clothes back on, we left the blankets spread out on the ground to dry in the sun that was now up pretty high.

Not wanting to get back in the hole unless our lives depended upon it, we lay spread-eagle on top of the ground next to the wall to soak up the sunshine.

About midday we got the word to move out to another location. Before leaving, I examined the slab and its pile of manure. I discovered that a hand pump was located next to the other wall so that water could be pumped over the wall and onto the manure. It was obvious that the pile was kept wet intentionally. Water was constantly draining out of the manure and over the open edges of the slab and was finally absorbed into the ground. This had probably been going on for several generations. I now knew the source of the water that was in our hole.

Troutman and I took a good dip, fully clothed, in the first stream that we came to. This got most of the odor from our clothing. We were cold and wet most of the day but by sundown were nearly dry again.

That was a miserable experience. But most of all, it was a very valuable learning experience. Never again would I dig within a hundred feet of a manure pile or building if I had a choice.

A Darby's Ranger, Almost

I entered the US Army in March of 1943. I received my basic infantry training in Fort Jackson, South Carolina. After our basic training was completed, we were placed in the army's replacement pool and began our journey to assignments to various combat units overseas. This involved processing through replacement depots in Africa and Italy.

As we were processed through these depots, we would become more and more separated from the friends we had trained with. In an effort to stay in touch, we would meet in front of the mess hall at the end of each day, at each new camp. By the time we reached the replacement camp in Italy, there were about ten of us that were still together. That first night in Italy, knowing that our next assignment would be a combat unit, we made a vow to do everything we could to be assigned to the same unit.

The next morning (being a private), I was assigned to work in the mess hall (known as KP duty) and was not finished until about 9:00 p.m. that night. As soon as I was off, I went to see my friends and learned that they had volunteered to join a ranger battalion. In keeping with our vow, I immediately reported to the first sergeant and asked that I be assigned to the ranger battalion that my friends had joined. The sergeant explained that he had no control over that. An officer from the Darby's Rangers had recruited my friends. He told me that the officer would be back the next day and that I could sign up for the rangers then. The rangers took their name from their commanding officer, Col. William O. Darby.

The next morning, at first muster, the first sergeant read an assignment list for replacements being sent to the Third Infantry Division. My name was on that list. When we were dismissed, I reported to the first sergeant and asked that I be taken off the list so that I could join the rangers. He said that the orders could not be changed and that I would be sent to the Third Division. I was assigned to Company H, Thirtieth Infantry Regiment, Third Infantry Division. That was in November of 1943. I served with the Third Division for the remainder of the war, ending in Salzburg, Austria, in May of 1945.

Portions of the above are important background for the following story.

The Third Division was one of two divisions to make the assault landings near Anzio, Italy, on January 22, 1944. The Anzio Beachhead landing was considered a success at the beginning. But the number of ships available for our support was limited because of Prime Minister Churchill's insistence that all but a limited number be sent to England to prepare for the Normandy invasion. Because the number of ships was limited, the Germans were able to build up opposition forces faster than could we. They had us outnumbered by the fifth day. This prevented the Allied forces from expanding the beachhead immediately.

By January 30, 1944, when this story takes place, the Germans were well prepared for our forthcoming attacks.

The Allied forces planned a major attack to begin in the early morning of January 30. The initial objective was to take and hold the town of Cisterna di Littoria, which was about a mile in front of our current defensive positions.

Two of Darby's ranger battalions were to move by stealth through the German lines to be in positions behind the enemy to aid elements of the Third Division in a frontal attack at daylight. These were the First and Third ranger battalions, the ranger battalions that my friends had joined.

I was manning a machine gun next to a bridge over which the rangers would pass as they moved out for their mission. The rangers began coming past my position about 0100. I got up on the road and walked with them for a short distance, looking for my friends. I did find two of them and was able to wish them success.

It was later learned that the Germans were aware of our plan and permitted the rangers to pass without opposition. They then formed a circle of infantry, tanks, and artillery around them. At daylight the rangers stormed out of a streambed where they had been waiting and were immediately engaged by the Germans. They were caught in a cross fire of small arms, tank, and artillery, all at point-blank range.

From our positions we could see the smoke and explosions but could do nothing to help. The rangers fought desperately and held out until almost midday.

Efforts to come to their rescue were blocked by the enemy's superiority in men, tanks, and artillery. The Fourth Ranger Battalion participated in the attempt to break through the Germans' defenses and was so decimated that it was no longer a fighting force.

Of the 780 men in the First and Third rangers, only seven returned.

Darby's Rangers were written off and never reactivated.

It was very difficult to watch and know that my friends from basic training were being killed without a chance. Had I not been put on KP the day they joined the rangers, I would have been there with them.

Koppelschloss

At our briefing, after boarding the LST in Naples, Italy, we were told that we would be awakened at midnight to load into LCVPs for a 2:00 a.m. landing on an undisclosed beach. We were advised to get as much sleep as we could.

Following that advice, I decided to hit the hammock about 8:00 p.m. I was, of course, very anxious about coming events. I had not yet been in combat and did not know what to expect or how I would perform.

I was not given to praying often but decided that maybe I might try one. My prayer was a very selfish one. I was to be the only benefactor. I then climbed into my hammock to get some sleep. But sleep would not come. The prayer had not relieved any of my anxiety.

I lay in the hammock thinking about home and my parents. I knew that they were praying for me constantly. Then it hit. There are many Christians in Germany. My mother was from Germany. My enemies' parents would be praying for them just as diligently as my parents were for me. Boy, did we have God boxed in!

I decided that frightened, selfish prayers were not going to get it done. I dialed in again and asked God to scrap my first request. I asked that he not favor me over my enemy, but to help me meet what trials were to come with courage and not be a disgrace. I promised to do my part by using my wits and brains that he had provided. I felt better and fell asleep in a few minutes.

A couple of weeks later, I had my first opportunity to examine a dead German soldier closely. I noticed the impression that was molded into his aluminum *koppelschloss* (belt buckle). It was an army-issue buckle that they all wore. In a circle around the center symbol were imprinted the words "Gott mit uns," God with us. As I looked at the buckle I remembered my thoughts aboard the LST. I was right. My enemy has as much right of access to God as I. I did not want to ever forget that, so I removed the soldier's *koppelschloss* and put it in my pocket. I wanted something to keep me reminded that my enemy and I were the same. Only the uniforms were different. I also wanted something to keep me from hating him. I would kill if I must, but I did not want it to be driven by hate.

I carried the *koppelschloss* in my right-front pocket from that moment on, until the war was over. I put it with my personal things and brought it home with me. It remained with my war souvenirs until May of 2001.

Jo and I were planning a trip to Europe to follow my trail in the war. In my planning, I learned of several annual events and ceremonies that took place in Europe at different times of the year. Other Third Division veterans had participated in them and told about them in our society newspaper.

There was one of particular interest to me. It was scheduled at a time that would fit into our schedule. It was a memorial service held annually at a monument near Jebsheim, France, near Colmar, where much vicious fighting took place. The monument has three sides, each side representing French, German, and American soldiers that fought there. The center of the monument is left open in the shape of a Christian cross.

They meet with the theme "Our Enemies Became Our Friends." They are committed to promoting peace in the world.

I had fought in the battles that took place there and decided that I wanted to attend the ceremonies. In writing to various people in France and Germany, I made contact with a German who was in the German Nineteenth Army that we fought against from the shores of France, up the Rhone Valley, across Germany and into Austria.

He seemed to be a very nice man, and I wanted to meet him. He told me that he would be at the ceremonies. I decided that I would take the *koppelschloss* with me and give it to him. It was time for it to go back home.

At the ceremonial dinner following the ceremonies at the Cross at Jebsheim, which is what they call the monument, I gave Albrecht Englert the *koppelschloss*. Through an interpreter, I explained how I took possession of it and why I had kept it. I wanted him to keep it on behalf of the soldier who wore it.

Albrecht was very pleased to accept the buckle, and in return, he removed a pin from his lapel and insisted that I take it. The commander of the Nineteenth Army had awarded the pin to him. It was for some honorable deed that he had performed in the war. I did not want to take something of that nature, but he would have it no other way.

Albrecht and I correspond regularly. We have exchanged a few experiences from the war.

Albrecht was a radio operator in the Nineteenth Army Headquarters. In that capacity, he was privy to many historical events as they unfolded. One story that he shared with me was his part in saving the lives of a group of fairly high-ranking German officers.

The incident took place a few days before the official surrender on May 8, 1945. This group of officers, appalled at the useless slaughter of their men and ours in a cause who's outcome was known, appealed to the top generals of the Nineteenth Army to permit them to surrender.

The appeal backfired. They were all court-martialed and found to be guilty of treason. They were sentenced to execution by firing squad. However, because the condemned were officers, the court-martial board did not have authority to carry out the executions without approval of the highest army command.

They brought their execution request to Albrecht to transmit to the higher command. Albrecht signaled his assistant to turn the transmitter's power to its lowest setting. His transmitter was a one-thousand-watt transmitter when at its highest setting. It could reach any station in Germany with no trouble. But at its lowest setting, its range was just a very few miles.

Albrecht sent the message. The generals stood behind him waiting for a reply. When no reply came back, they ordered Albrecht to send it again, which he did. Still there was no reply. Several more attempts were made, but none brought a reply.

The generals finally gave up, thinking that perhaps something tragic had happened at the high command headquarters. A few days later, Germany surrendered, and there was no legal authority to carry out the executions.

Beyond a doubt, Albrecht's actions saved the lives of those good officers. In so doing, he put his own life on the line. If the generals had gotten wise, Albrecht would have surely been executed with the officers.

Anzio Shep

Normally, we only think of people casualties in a war. Seldom do we measure war's cost in innocent animals.

Hardly a day of combat passed without my witnessing the death and maiming of animals. They were farm animals, wild animals, and household pets. The Germans used a number of horse-drawn wagons and artillery pieces. These animals became targets of war but still were innocent in my mind.

Anzio Beachhead was by far the worst for animal slaughter that I witnessed. For four months, the beachhead perimeter was a fan-shaped piece of real estate. It measured about ten miles along the shore and was about eight miles deep at the deepest point.

This area was mostly flat farmland. In addition to the usual assortment of farm animals you expect to find in farm country was a flock of sheep. The size of this flock was estimated at the beginning to be as many as two hundred.

The owner of these sheep obviously was no longer tending them. However, a large sheep dog was still faithfully at his post. We called him Shep. The sheep were forever getting caught in the war's exchanges of artillery and small-arms fire.

Whenever the flock was scattered after being caught in our cross fire, Shep would go right to work rounding them up and calming them down. If the sheep got caught in a minefield, Shep would remember the area and would guide the sheep away from it after that.

Weeks went by, the flock grew smaller and smaller, but faithful Shep was still on the job guiding and calming them. And then one day, Shep was no longer seen. Our only conclusion was that he was finally a casualty himself. The sheep, now fewer than fifty in number, began to wander in ever smaller and scattered groups until eventually they were no more.

Somewhere in heaven is a beautiful sheepdog with a CMH medal hanging around his neck.

Ringside Seat

In the early weeks of the Anzio Beachhead campaign, there was a real battle for dominance of the skies. The Allies finally won that battle, and during the latter weeks we were only occasionally attacked by enemy planes.

One morning in February our positions were attacked by a German ME 109 fighter plane. It came in low strafing our positions. After its first run, it climbed to a minimum maneuvering altitude and made a 180-degree turn and was dropping in for another pass. Before he reached our positions a second time, a British Spitfire fighter plane that was patrolling the beachhead came in from above to intervene in the ME 109's plan.

With the Spitfire on its tail, the ME 109 broke off from its strafing run and turned upward to gain altitude and to attempt to get above and behind the Spitfire. Thus began a very exciting dogfight above us.

We had ringside seats to the best show of the day. There is no doubt as to which side we were on. Our dogfaces along the entire front were yelling and cheering for the Spitfire. And as was expected, we could hear the Germans in their positions yelling and cheering whenever the ME 109 gained the advantage.

This dogfight lasted about ten minutes until finally the Spitfire got into great position and opened fire with all its guns. The bullets were on target, and the ME 109 began to trail smoke. Then we saw a parachute open as the German pilot escaped the burning plane.

Of course the cheering stopped on the German side while we dogfaces went wild. My foxhole mate, Chester Borowski, and I were yelling and slapping each other in glee when I changed my gaze from man and parachute to the ME 109. To my horror, the burning plane was coming in on a steep angle and headed dead straight for our foxhole.

I pointed to the plane, and Chester saw it too. Our celebration came to an abrupt end. To abandon our foxhole in broad daylight would be suicidal, but staying put appeared to be worse. Just as we decided to run for it, the plane did a barrel roll to the left and crashed about twenty yards from our hole. A hot blast swept over us as the plane exploded into flames.

Our attention was then turned back to the pilot and parachute. Both sides at the front were calling for the wind to bring him to their side of the line. For a while it was not clear where he would land. Finally a gust of wind brought him down close to our frontline positions. Two riflemen darted out and took him prisoner. The enemy did not fire because they did not want to risk killing their man.

That was a very exciting show that we chattered about for days afterward.

Beachhead Spies

At the beginning of the war, Italy was an ally of Germany, and we were at war with both countries. During the fighting in Sicily, Italy surrendered and supposedly became our ally. But there were many die-hard Fascists in Italy that did not come over to our side.

After the landings at Anzio, civilians were allowed to stay if they chose to. Many stayed.

After a few weeks on Anzio Beachhead, our intelligence people began to suspect spies in our midst. The Germans knew too much of our plans too soon.

A beachhead-wide search and investigation was launched. The search discovered a two-way radio in the cellar of a civilian-occupied farmhouse. The woman's clothesline was the antenna. When she hung her clothes on the line, it was the signal for the Germans to get on their frequency. The spies had a message to send. It worked well, because the Germans held all of the high ground and had visual observation of the entire beachhead.

The spies became suspects when it was noticed that the woman often hung out clothes on rainy days.

The spies were caught and dealt with.

After that, all civilians were evacuated whether they wanted to leave or not.

It is strongly believed that this spy group was responsible for the details of the first attack on Cisterna being compromised to the Germans. The Germans were aware of the details of that plan and permitted two ranger battalions to pass through their positions at night and then surrounded them. Both battalions were annihilated.

(See "A Darby's Ranger, Almost.")

Party Line

After about two months, Anzio Beachhead became stalemated. The Germans discovered that they were not going to drive us into the Mediterranean as Hitler had ordered. We did not have the resources to break out.

This began a period of patrol activities to test for weaknesses, and of small-scale attacks to improve positions. Both sides attempted to gain ground without fighting for it by digging new positions at night a few yards in front of present positions.

Finally, our lines, in some places, became so close that we could hear each other milling around or talking at night, even if we spoke in lowered voices. Some of our food rations came in cartons secured with wire bands. The enemy could hear the snap of the wire when it was cut. This told them that we were out of our foxholes distributing supplies. We quickly learned to wrap the wire in cloth and to cut the wire slowly through the cloth. This technique would safely muffle the sound.

We had to be extremely careful not to establish predictable schedules and patterns. The enemy would take advantage of our timetable and rake our positions with rockets, artillery, mortars and machineguns when they suspected that we would be out of our holes. Every night, ammunition, food rations and other essentials were brought forward and distributed. It was necessary that these activities take place at widely different times.

For a period of time my section was assigned to positions that were at the most forward position on the beachhead. Our defenses made a very pronounced curvature at this point.

Late one night, my foxhole partner, Chester Borowski, and I heard a strange sound. It gradually grew louder as the source got closer. The sound was a "squeak squawk", "squeak squawk", "squeak squawk". We recognized the sound. It was the sound of a metal spool turning on a heavy metal wire through its center hub. It was someone laying communication wire for telephones. But, was it German or American?

Borowski and I decided to check it out. We put ourselves in the wire layer's path and waited. Just before he reached our ambush point, two riflemen from Company G nabbed him.

It was a German who, because of the nearness of our positions to his, and because of the bend in the front lines, he had unwittingly passed through our defenses and was passing behind us.

His captors ordered him to continue laying the wire and directed him to the Company G command post where the Company Commander hooked on his own phone and listened in on the "party line". We were told that this was good for about a day and a half. It ended when the Germans got wise and cut the line leading to our positions.

Paintbrushes, Stencils, and Blue and White Paint

(More about Iron Mike O'Daniel)

Lt. Gen. Lucien K. Truscott commanded the Third Infantry Division in North Africa, Sicily, Italy, and during the early days on Anzio Beachhead. A few weeks after the Anzio invasion, the corps commander, Lt. Gen. John P. Lucas, was replaced by General Truscott. As corps commander, Truscott had command of all units on the beachhead, including the British units.

General Truscott moved the corps command headquarters from the cellars in Anzio to a two-story farmhouse within a half mile of the most advanced positions. From there he could observe firsthand almost the entire frontline perimeter.

He placed Gen. John W. O'Daniel, who had been his assistant division commander, in command of the Third Infantry Division. General Truscott and General O'Daniel were cut from the same cloth, as the saying goes.

Known by his troops as "Iron Mike," General O'Daniel was, like Truscott, a very aggressive leader. He was always close to where the fiercest fighting was. It was not uncommon for his troops to see him in areas of great danger.

Iron Mike knew the importance of maintaining high morale. His motive for staying close to the fighting was to enable him to make better and quicker command decisions, but he also knew that it gave a great boost to morale.

Soon after taking command, Iron Mike made an important morale-boosting decision. He acquired paintbrushes, Third Division insignia stencils, and blue and white paint. He had these distributed to every Third Division soldier with orders to paint the Third Division insignia on both sides of their helmets.

With the order, he explained that the Third Division was the best damn unit in the US Army, and he wanted the Krauts to know that it was "the Blue and White Devils" that were kicking their butts. Normally, units prefer to conceal identities lest the knowledge be of advantage to the enemy. It gave us a great sense of pride to know that our commander had such a high opinion of us. It was a tremendous morale booster.

The Third Division did not name itself "the Blue and White Devils." That is the name the Germans gave the division back in Sicily.

At Anzio Beachhead, replacement troops would arrive almost daily. The first requirement of each soldier who was being assigned to the Third Division was to paint the blue and white insignia on their helmets, with Iron Mike's above explanation. Whenever it was possible, Iron Mike met the incoming replacements and gave them the message in person.

From that beginning to the end of the war, the Third Division insignia was on our helmets.

Anzio Annie

Almost everyone that knows much about Anzio Beachhead has heard of Anzio Annie.

Unfortunately Anzio Annie was not a voluptuous female. It was a very large artillery piece that fired a shell 280 millimeters (11 inches) in diameter. The gun was mounted on a railroad car and was moved in and out of tunnels some twenty to thirty miles from the beachhead. It was capable of hurling a 550-pound shell a distance of 38 miles. Actually, the Germans had more than one of these poised around the beachhead.

The Germans had another, even larger, railroad gun that had limited use at Anzio Beachhead. It could hurl a 16" diameter 1,600-pound shell even farther than the 280mm gun. Its use was limited because it could fire only one round per day. It had to be lowered and allowed to cool or the barrel would bend from overheating. Both guns were dubbed Anzio Annie.

However, it was the 280mm gun that did most of the firing and was more famous.

This huge cannon was capable of reaching any spot on the beachhead, and during the four-month period that the campaign lasted, few places on the beachhead had not been targeted.

Because of its great range, its projectiles reached a very high altitude before returning to earth. If the beachhead happened to be quiet at the time it was fired, the sound could be heard at the frontline. But because of the time required for the sound to travel the twenty to thirty miles between the gun and our positions, the projectile was well on its way to impact by the time we would hear it. At night, the flash could often be seen. This provided more warning than in the daylight. Following the sound of firing, we would listen for the sound of the projectile as it climbed higher and higher. It made a soft whispering sound (*whooah-whooah-whooah*) with small pulsations.

The only way to know if you were going to be in the impact area was if the sound suddenly stopped. If the sound stopped, you **were** in the impact area. Two seconds after the sound stopped, the shell would impact. We called it the two-second warning. One second to realize that the sound had stopped. One second to hit the ground.

This phenomenon was created because of the long range and great height of the trajectory. The muzzle velocity was 3,700 feet per second. The shell's velocity would be diminished by the restraints of gravity to about 2,600 feet per second as it reached its high point. It would then gather speed as it turned downward toward the target. By the time it reached the ground, it would be back close to its original velocity. Its average velocity for the entire flight would be just over 3,000 feet per second, or about three times the speed of sound. At sea level, sound travels about 1,040 feet per second.

Therefore, even though the projectile traveled a longer path than the sound, it would still arrive well ahead of its own sound. Actually the shell would impact the target at about the same time that the sound from the highest point in its trajectory was arriving at the impact area. This gave a false sense of security. From the sound, one was given the impression that the projectile was still high above the ground when, actually, it was only a few seconds from impact.

I am certain that scientists can explain the sound cutoff phenomenon. My guess is that the shock wave surrounding the projectile canceled out its distant sound waves so that the distant flight sounds arriving at the target area were blocked by this shock wave when the shell was near impact. While I cannot claim to understand it, I can attest to the fact that it occurred.

If the shell was destined for impact a substantial distance beyond or to the left or right of our positions, the sound would fade somewhat, but not stop, and build right back again as it plunged to earth. In this case we could hear the projectile all the way to impact. Being aware of this phenomenon was just another tool for survival and was quickly learned.

I would always tell the new men arriving from the States that in combat you do not live and learn. You learn and live.

One of the 280mm versions of the gun "Anzio Annie" captured after the breakout from Anzio Beachhead. (courtesy dogfacesoldiers'org)

Get Off the Beach

The Third Division had received much specialized training for amphibious assault landings prior to leaving the US to invade North Africa in November of 1942. Because of this, it was frequently called upon for amphibious operations. The Third Division made a total of four amphibious landings during the war. My battalion, Second Battalion, Thirtieth Infantry, made six amphibious landings. In addition to four with the division, it made two more battalion-strength landings behind the enemy lines in Sicily.

The Third Division always resumed training for amphibious assault landings whenever it was not committed to active combat. The necessity to get off the beach was constantly drilled into us. During the critique that followed every practice landing, our battalion commander, Lt. Col. Lyle W. Bernard, had his own unique way of making this point to us.

His favorite expression was "horseshit". He ran the two syllables together so that they came out as one syllable, "horseshit". All the troops referred to him as Horseshit Bernard. He knew this and never seemed to mind.

He was never satisfied with the speed with which we got off the beach. At the beginning of every critique, he would say, "What I saw out there was a lot of Horseshit. You were too slow getting off the beach. That's pure Horseshit".

You may ask, "What about the enemy machine guns?" I say, "Horseshit. Get off the beach." "What about the minefields, sir?" I say, "Horseshit. Get off the beach." "But, sir, what about the enemy tanks?" I say, "Horseshit. Get off the beach."

Then he would remind us that the beach was the most vulnerable place to be. All of the enemy weapons had fields of fire covering the beach. Mortars and artillery pieces were always preaimed to cover the beach. Enemy planes always flew paralleling and in line with the beach in bombing and strafing runs. Staying on the beach was worse than charging the enemy's positions.

This became painfully true at Normandy on June 6, 1944. Some units sustained unusually high casualties because they were slow getting off the beach.

The last time I saw Colonel Bernard over there (I have met him a few times at our reunions since the war) was on February 19, 1944. He had been severely wounded and was in a large bomb crater giving orders to his field commanders on his radio. A medic was tending his wound and trying to persuade him to allow himself to be evacuated so that he could get better attention.

His reply to the medic was "Horseshit. This fight ain't over yet. Horseshit."

My section continued forward behind the rifle company, and I could still hear him using his favorite word until we were out of earshot.

Col. Lyle W. Bernard, Commander, Second Battalion,
Thirtieth Infantry Regiment, Third Infantry Division

Machine gun bullet through his lung March 19, 1944,
sent him back to the States for the duration.
(courtesy of dogfacesoldiers.org)

(See memoir "Get Off the Beach")

ALTEO

On February 19, 1944, our battalion commander, Lt. Col. Lyle W. Bernard, was wounded and evacuated. Lt. Col. Woodrow W. Armstrong was given command of the Second Battalion.

Soon after taking command, Colonel Armstrong decided that the Second Battalion needed a battle cry. He wanted something the men could shout as they left their line of departure and charged the enemy positions, something that would inspire comradeship and unity, and that would be intimidating to the enemy (ha ha).

He sent down word that there would be a contest to find a suitable battle cry. He would accept suggestions for one week. Only enlisted men could participate. A panel of two officers and two enlisted men would review all entries and determine a winner.

The winner would receive a thirty-day furlough to the US of A. A large number of men sent in their suggestions. After the end of the one-week entry period, the review panel met and made its selection. They chose "ALTEO." Pronounced: *al* as in *Albert*, *tay* is in *take*, and *o* as in *oh*.

A-All
L-Loyal
T-To
E-Each
O-Other

The driver of the supply jeep that was to deliver supplies to the winner's company that night was instructed to carry the good news to the winner. He was further instructed to bring the winner back to Battalion Headquarters to begin processing of his furlough papers. On that particular night, supplies were being brought up between 0100 and 0200 hours.

Unfortunately, the winner had been on a reconnaissance patrol into enemy territory. The patrol was discovered as it was sneaking back through enemy positions on its return from the mission. (I have to refer to him as the winner because I cannot recall his name.) Enemy machine guns opened fire on the patrol, killing the contest winner. This happened about an hour before the jeep arrived.

Instead of a ride back in the jeep to begin a trip to the States, the winner rode back on the hood of the jeep for burial. He was then turned over to a grave registration team, which is the military unit that records the necessary paperwork and buries the dead.

The entire battalion was saddened by this tragic event. To my knowledge, the battle cry was seldom, if ever, used in combat. However, in noncombat situations, ALTEO was sometimes used to signify comradeship, and/or support, for a fellow soldier. Even today, at our reunions, ALTEO is used on occasion in the manner stated in the preceding sentence.

One Tiger, Three Shermans

In many instances, Germany's equipment was superior to ours. The best example of that was in their armor (tanks). Their most impressive tank, Mark VI, also known as Tiger, was a monster weighing more than seventy-six tons.

The armor plating in the front was nearly eight inches thick and sloped so that our tank shells just glanced off it. We had nothing that would penetrate the front. Our tanks could only attack it from the sides or rear.

It featured an 88mm cannon. This cannon fired projectiles at 3,800 to 4,200 feet per second, depending upon the type of ammunition. High-explosive shells were in the 3,800-feet-per-second range. Armor piercing rounds were in the 4,200-feet-per-second range. For a benchmark, consider the fact that this is four times the speed of sound. Not only does the shell arrive ahead of the sound of the cannon, it is ahead of its own sound that it makes traveling through the air. If you hear it, it has passed you.

One morning, on Anzio Beachhead, a German Tiger tank made its presence known. It was hidden somewhere in a stand of trees and brush about one thousand yards to our left front. It was just firing on targets of opportunity. It being well hidden, we were not able to get an exact fix on its position so that we could place heavy artillery on it. Also, it kept changing position. This made it even more difficult to spot.

Finally, about midmorning, three of our General Sherman medium tanks appeared from a group of buildings about three hundred yards to the left and rear of my position. These tanks began moving along an unpaved road in the general direction of the Tiger tank. The land between our tanks and the Tiger was flat farmland. The Germans had to be watching them. I watched in disbelief as they kept rolling along at about half speed. Had they not been warned of the presence of the Tiger?

Suddenly there were two explosions less than a second apart. The first explosion was the Tiger's cannon when it fired. The second explosion was when the shell struck our lead tank. The lead tank stopped dead, and the surviving occupants began to exit it.

Immediately, the second tank broke to the right and crossed the shallow roadway ditch and headed into the field. At the same time, the third tank broke to the left and headed for a masonry farmhouse that was very close to the road.

The second tank had barely crossed the ditch when, again, there were two explosions within a second. The second tank was put out of action, and the survivors began exiting.

The third tank succeeded in taking cover behind the masonry farmhouse. Our tankers had no intention of taking on the Tiger. They only hoped to survive.

There was a long wait, maybe as much as ten minutes, our tank did not move, and the Tiger did nothing. Just as I was feeling good that at least one of our tanks was safe, then again, there were two rapid explosions. I looked to the farmhouse and saw a gray dust cloud rising from the masonry structure. Black smoke was already coming from our tank, and men were scrambling to get out.

The crew of the Tiger had grown tired of waiting for our tank to show itself and had fired an armor-piercing round right through the building and through our Sherman.

After witnessing that episode, I had the greatest respect for our tankers who had to go up against tanks like that.

Tiger Tank

Note that the gun is level to the horizon. In this position the shell would reach the target in 0.375 second and only drop 2.25 feet at a range of 500 yards (1,500 feet, or 0.3 of a mile). At a range of 1,000 yards (3,000 feet, or 0.6 of a mile) the shell would reach the target in 0.75 second and drop only nine feet. The gunner was able to "bore-sight" this weapon i.e., simply look through the barrel prior to loading a shell and center the muzzle on his target, load and pull the lanyard.

A Tragic Night

What does it take to survive in combat? Mostly luck! However, experience and composure are great allies on the front line. Some soldiers survive months of combat, while others may only survive a few minutes.

Soldiers with experience react better and make fewer mistakes. Therefore, the longer one survives, the greater is his chance of continued survival. The story related below is a good example of how panic can reduce one's longevity on the front.

Background Info

The Germans used rockets a lot to supplement artillery and mortars. An incoming artillery shell gives you, at most, a one-second warning before it hits. A mortar comes in so silently that you get no warning. But a rocket gives you ample warning if you are alert and paying attention, especially at night. In the daytime, if you are looking, you can see the trail of smoke as the rocket rises above the horizon. At night it is much easier to see them because of their fiery tail.

We always had two men assigned the responsibility to watch for rockets and to sound the alarm if they spotted any headed for our positions. It is easy to determine if you are in their line of flight. If the smoke trails or fire trails are vertical, you are in their path. The only unknown is the distance they are set for.

One night in February 1944, we received two new men as replacements for losses we had taken a day or two before. The new men had no prior combat experience. After interviewing the two replacements, I assigned them to a foxhole that had been occupied by the men they were replacing. In my briefing, I went into great detail about our rocket warning system. I warned them to stay near their foxhole if they chose to get out to stretch. I pointed out that they would have only five to ten seconds to take cover if rockets were on the way.

We received the two men about ten o'clock that night. It was around midnight when rockets were spotted and the warning was given. Everyone except the two new men took quick refuge in their foxholes. I heard the new men running around shouting to each other in panic. They couldn't find their foxhole in the dark. Unfortunately for them, our positions were the chosen target this time. About six rockets struck our positions in rapid succession, and the new men were no longer shouting.

I investigated and found them both dead within a few feet of their foxhole. This was a case where luck was not involved, panic was. Who's to say that these two wouldn't have survived the war if they had only remained calm and reacted intelligently?

I witnessed several other incidences where men became casualties because of their own carelessness or panic. I chose to relate this incident as an example only because these deaths were so clearly avoidable.

My Encounter with a Flare

Anzio Beachhead, Mid-April 1944

January through March was a time of much fighting. The Germans were trying to drive us into the Mediterranean Sea. We were fighting to hold on to the ground we had and to expand and improve our positions as much as possible. By mid-April both sides were ready to call it a stalemate. This began a period of mutual harassment from both sides, consisting of small-scale attacks, artillery and mortar bombardments, and much patrol penetrations into the other's territory.

It was during this stalemate period that I had the following experience: One night, around 1:00 a.m., the telephone communication from my machine gun position to my platoon leader's position was lost. I left my position to find the cause and to restore our communication.

It was a very dark but clear night. Every star in the sky was visible and bright. To find the break in the wires, I crawled on hands and knees, letting the telephone wires slide through my hand as I moved. As I was searching for the break, I was keenly aware of two possibilities: (1) the wire was cut by an artillery or mortar shell, or (2) an enemy patrol had cut the wires and was prepared to ambush anyone coming to repair it. With that thought in mind, I proceeded very cautiously.

After proceeding some fifty yards, I came to a clean break in the wires at the edge of a shell crater. After a few minutes of searching in the darkness, I found the other ends of the wires and began splicing them back together.

In order to see anything at all in the darkness, I had to lie on my back and work above my head. With the stars as a background, I was able to see just well enough to perform the task.

At one point, while working on the repair, an enemy flare suddenly lit up the entire area where I lay. I instantly froze in position, knowing that even the slightest movement would be detected. But on the other hand, if I did not move, there was a chance I would not be seen.

It was one of their largest flares. It was suspended by a parachute. It was directly above me. The air was cold and still, and the flare was not drifting, but coming straight for the spot where I lay.

When it was about twenty feet above the ground, it was evident that if it did not change course, it would land right on me. A burning flare can burn a hole right through you, so I had to have a plan. If I had to move, I was prepared to roll away from the enemy positions at the last split second. By letting the flare land between us, the enemy would not be able to see through the glare. On the other hand, if it landed behind me, I would be silhouetted by the flare, and they would surely see me.

When it was about five feet above me, and just as I was going to roll away, a gust of air sprang up and moved the flare toward the enemy positions. It landed about three feet from me, and I did not have to move. I remained motionless another thirty seconds while the flared burned itself out.

After recovering from being blinded by the flare, I completed the splice and returned to my position and thanked God for the timely gust of air.

Pfc. Myles F. Pratico

My brother, Frank, and I were inducted together and were sent to Fort Jackson, South Carolina, for basic training. We were assigned to the 106th Infantry Division. I was in the 422nd Regiment. Frank was in the 424th Regiment. We were able to see each other often when off duty. From my visits to Frank's barracks, I got to know many of his friends. His closest friend was Myles Pratico.

Myles was of Italian ancestry and was from New York City. His hair was thick and very black.

Fast forward to Anzio Beachhead, February 1944.

One morning in late February, my battalion, Second Battalion, Thirtieth Regiment, was moving through a staging area where First Battalion, Thirtieth Regiment, was relaxing. I noticed a First Battalion soldier that stood out from the others because of his snow-white hair. As I got closer, I thought that I knew him but could not quite identify him.

I also noticed that he was looking at me as though he recognized me. When we were about twenty feet apart, the soldier said, "Hi, Al." It was then that I recognized him. It was Myles Pratico.

I broke formation to stop and visit with him for a couple of minutes. We compared notes about things that had happened to us since Fort Jackson. I wanted to ask him about his hair but was hesitant for fear that he might be sensitive about it.

Finally, I got the courage and asked him what had happened to his hair. He said that he didn't know. He said that in a period of a few days after landing on the beachhead it had just changed from black to white.

I wondered if it might have been caused by some chemical changes brought on from the stress of combat. I guess I'll never know.

We said goodbye, and I hurried to catch up with my unit. I never saw Myles again, so I do not know if the color ever returned.

In *The History of the Third Infantry Division in WWII*, he is reported as being a prisoner of war. He must have been captured soon after our meeting. Since we were in the same regiment, our paths would have crossed occasionally if he had stayed around for any significant time.

If he were captured in the early fighting, as I assume, he would have been in German PW camps for more than a year. If he fared no better than most of our PWs that we liberated in April and May of 1945, his situation was worse than being in combat, in my opinion. I do hope that he survived the ordeal.

I received the following e-mail from Myles's daughter:

Hello Mr. Brown,

My name is Leslie (Pratico) Keefe. I am Myles F. Pratico's daughter. My dad spoke very little of the war because of the trauma he endured. I now have a 13 year old son, who never met my dad and is writing an essay on being an American Citizen for a local VFW organization. I have told Joseph my dad's story many times. I was just on line and googled my dad in hopes of finding something of his war experience. I just finished reading your Memories of World War II, Dogface Soldiers Memoirs.

I would love to speak with you and find out more of my dad's experience and I want to share with you the bit of information he was able to confide in me concerning his capture and escape. As I mentioned, he could not speak about his experience but at the end of this life, which was taken too soon at age 68 of cancer, he did tell me some details of his captivity and dramatic escape from the war camp.

I would like to speak with you in person if possible. Please do call me.

I have always wanted to write about my father's war experience. Our conversation may be a place to start.

I look forward to hearing from you.

All the very best,
Leslie Keefe

Note: I called Leslie and had a very long, interesting conversation with her. Among other things, Leslie confirmed that Myles's hair did return to its natural black color. Apparently, the whitening was a temporary condition brought on by the stress and anxieties of combat. Al

Sacrificial Lambs

After much activity during the first six or seven weeks on Anzio Beachhead, the fighting subsided substantially. Both sides became content to just hold the lines where they were. This began a period of mostly patrol activity with an occasional "limited objective" attack.

It was near the beginning of this phase that our machine guns were in positions along a creek bed. The guns were positioned about five feet back from the creek and about thirty yards from each other. The creek provided an obstacle for the enemy in the event of an attack. The downside was that an enemy patrol could use the creek bed to get dangerously close to our positions without being detected.

The creek varied from ten to fifteen feet in width and was six to ten feet deep. Following heavy rains in the nearby mountains, the creek bed would run nearly full. During dry periods it only maintained a foot or two of water that ran in a subchannel pretty much in the center of the creek bed. It was possible to walk along this creek and avoid the water by staying just outside the subchannel.

The following incident happened during a period when this creek was at minimum flow.

It was late at night after both sides had settled in for what each hoped would be a quiet night. I was standing watch at one of our machine gun positions when I heard what sounded like rocks falling into the water. I was well aware of our vulnerability to enemy patrols and was immediately alert.

We always kept a good supply of hand grenades beside the machine gun. I picked up one of the grenades in my right hand and inserted a finger from the left hand into the ring that you pull before tossing the grenade.

The first sounds that I heard seemed to be twenty or thirty feet from me. In a few seconds I heard another rock go into the water. I dared not act too quickly. This could very well be one of our patrols returning from a mission.

I gave a challenge and got more rocks in the water in response. I gave a second challenge, louder than the first. The second challenge only produced scuffling of feet and more rocks in the water. The sounds were closer each time. I gave a third challenge with the same results as the first two. By now the sounds were almost directly in front of me.

It was time to act. I pulled the pin on the grenade I was holding and lobbed it into the creek. I followed the first grenade with three or four others as rapidly as I could.

The explosions of my grenades brought the front lines to life. Both sides thought that they were being attacked and opened fire at nothing in particular. This firing spread in both directions from our sector until almost the entire beachhead front was a blaze of tracers. The firing continued for about five minutes and gradually subsided to just an occasional shot, and then finally, all was quiet again.

Of course, Troutman, who was asleep in the hole with me, was awake in an instant. He grabbed the machine gun to open fire. But I stopped him and explained what had happened. We both listened for more sounds of activity in the creek, but none came.

Finally, in the gray light of dawn, I ventured out of the hole to see what might be in the creek. I saw five or six hapless sheep, victims of my hand grenades.

These were some of the few sheep remaining from a flock of sheep that were wandering and grazing over the battlefield from the beginning. (See my story entitled "Anzio Shep.")

Walla from Walla Walla

Sgt. Louis J. Walla was from Walla Walla, Washington. This is no joke. You will find Sergeant Walla listed on page 531 of *The History of the Third Infantry Division in WWII*. If you check a map of the USA, you will find Walla Walla, Washington, about five miles north of the Washington-Oregon border and about thirty miles north of Pendleton, Oregon.

His mail with Walla Walla, Washington, return addresses was our confirmation of the validity of his claim.

Sergeant Walla took great pride in announcing to all replacements that he was Sergeant Walla from Walla Walla, Washington.

In case you haven't guessed, we called him Walla Walla Walla. For the sake of this story, I'll just call him Walla.

Walla came over with the division. He participated in the assault landings in North Africa November 8, 1942, and all of the divisions battles in Africa, Sicily, and Italy up to the time of this story.

Walla was the self-appointed morale booster of the First Platoon, Company H, Thirtieth Infantry. He never seemed to take anything seriously and would turn seemingly bad situations into something to grin about.

Early one morning on Anzio Beachhead, the Germans decided to begin our day with a breakfast wake-up call. They bombarded our positions with a ten-minute artillery barrage.

At the time, Walla was in a foxhole near the one that Chester Borowski and I shared. He was alone because his partner had gone on R & R for a few days. After it appeared that the Germans were going to give us a rest, Walla called out to us. We cautiously raised our heads above ground and looked in Walla's direction. He was much too exposed for my comfort, and he was pointing as he spoke.

He said, "One," and pointed to a shell hole that was very close to the SW corner of his position. Then he pointed to another shell hole very near the NW corner of his position and said, "Two." Then he pointed to a third shell hole near the NE corner of his hole and said, "Three." Finally, pointing to a fourth shell hole very close to the SE corner of his position he said, "Four."

It was obvious that all four of these shell holes were the result of the bombardment that had just ended. Steam was still rising from the moist earth that had been heated from the explosions.

After pointing out the four near misses, he was laughing as he said, "All I need is one in the middle and I'll have the five of spades." Chester and I were not as amused as Walla was.

The next morning the Germans sent their wake-up call a bit earlier, about two hours before daylight. Right in the middle of a series of shell explosions all around our position we heard someone yell, "SPOON," and into our laps came Walla, in a headfirst dive. ("Spoon" was Walla's warning to hit the dirt whenever he thought it would be prudent to do so.)

To say that Chester and I were surprised would be a substantial understatement. I asked Walla what the hell he thought he was doing. He replied that he had just decided to drop in for breakfast with us. He added that he was getting lonesome in the foxhole by himself. I said that he was welcome, but I thought that it would have been wiser to wait for the bombardment to end. He replied that he thought his timing was perfect.

Anyway, as soon as the shelling stopped, we decided to eat so that Walla could get back to his hole before daylight. Chester heated some water on the one-burner Coleman that we had. Chester shared his canteen cup of coffee with Walla. I did not drink coffee. I popped a tea bag in my cup. Since Walla didn't bring his own rations, we shared ours.

As the sky began to lighten in the east, we suggested to Walla that he should get back to his hole before it got too light. Walla replied, "I'm not going back to that hole. I'm going to dig another one tonight." We asked him what was wrong with the one he had been in for several days now. His answer was "I got my five of spades."

I asked, "What in the hell are you saying?" At this point he informed us that a shell had landed between his legs but did not explode. Being the joker that he was, I found it hard to believe him. I crawled to his hole and looked in. In the gray light of near dawn, I saw a 75mm shell half buried in the bottom of his hole.

Chester and I welcomed him for the day and helped him dig another hole as soon as it was dark that night.

Walla was wounded on the breakout from the beachhead. His wounds were not life threatening, but serious enough for a ticket back to Walla Walla.

Long after his departure, his spirit of non-surrender stayed with me.

A Very Bad Night

Fighting was somewhat limited on Anzio Beachhead from the landings on January 22 through February 2, 1944. Both sides were primarily concerned with containment and buildup of forces.

February 3 through March 3 was a month of very intense fighting. The Allied forces were ordered to break out of the beachhead and cut Highways 6 and 7. These highway routes were the enemy's main supply routes to the Casino Front that was south of Anzio. Cutting these supply lines would be a major catastrophe to the German armies blocking Allied advances along that front.

Because of this severe threat to his supply lines, and his rear areas in general, the enemy had to give first priority to eliminating the beachhead threat. *Adolf* Hitler ordered his forces to drive us into the sea.

Both sides were equally determined to accomplish their mission. The Germans made several serious penetrations into Allied-held territory during this period. Each penetration was immediately driven back before a major breakthrough could develop.

It was during fighting to eliminate enemy gains that the following incident occurred. On February 29, the enemy launched a full-scale attack against positions held by the 509th Parachute Battalion, driving it back one thousand five hundred yards and taking possession of some very critical high ground. The Second Battalion, Thirtieth Infantry (my battalion), was thrown into the breach to regain the lost ground. Company G and Company F were the assault companies, with Company E in reserve. My machine gun section was assigned to support Company G.

By nightfall, the Second Battalion had regained one thousand yards of the lost ground but was now in front of friendly units on either side. The enemy had thrown in fresh units and was attacking both flanks to our rear. They intended to isolate us.

Company E and the 509th Parachute Battalion were committed to deal with this threat. We were given orders to dig in and hold for the night.

As Chester Borowski and I were digging our foxhole, we heard a wounded German soldier calling out for help. We looked in the direction of the cries for help and saw the soldier about fifty yards from us, waving an arm in the air. We decided to help him. We approached him very cautiously, keeping him covered with our weapons. When we got to him, we saw that he was badly wounded. He had a compound fracture of his right leg between the knee and hip. There was no way that he could walk, not even with assistance.

I noted that this soldier was a private even though he was probably forty years old. This was older than most infantry privates. The older men normally are at least noncommissioned officers or commissioned officers. I wondered if he was from one of the countries the Germans had occupied. It was common for Germany to make men from captive nations fight in German units while their families were held hostage.

Together, we dragged the soldier to within a few feet of the hole we were digging. He cried out in pain with every movement. We made him as comfortable as we could and got back to our digging. After all, a counterattack could come at any time, and we had to be ready for it if it came.

Shortly after dark it began to rain. The temperature was only a few degrees above freezing. It was not going to be a good night.

Chester and I dug without letup until about 10:00 p.m., at which time we were finally satisfied with our foxhole. All the while, the German soldier was crying out in pain. There was very little that we could do for him. With Company E and the paratroopers engaging the enemy to our rear, it was not possible for litter teams from our battalion medical company to get through. We could not even evacuate our own wounded.

Before settling in the hole with Chester, I checked on our "guest." We had left him on his back, and the rain was pounding in his face. I rolled him over until he was facedown. This caused him great pain, and his screams tore through me. I wondered if I had done the right thing.

Chester and I settled in for the night, wrapped in our blankets for warmth and protection from the rain. All the while, without letup, our "guest" continued his cries of pain. Finally he began to beg us to shoot him, "Kamarad, ksheisten mich, kamarad, ksheisten mich." When we did not, he began to beg us to give him a gun, "Kamarad, pistole mich, kamarad, pistole mich."

This continued until about 2:00 a.m. Then there was an explosion very near our position. My first thought was that it was a mortar shell and that it was the beginning of an enemy attack. But there were no other explosions. An attack would not be preceded by one mortar round. Then

I realized that our "guest" was quiet, and I smelled burned flesh. Our friend had found a way. We had not searched him when we "rescued" him. In an inside pocket of his overcoat was a grenade. He had managed to reach it and pull the firing pin.

A Foxhole View of the Air War

This is written to honor and acknowledge our brave airmen of WWII. Their casualty rate was second only to the infantry. When you factor in time of exposure, their casualty rate was the highest (per hour of exposure) of any other branch of service.

From our frontline positions in Italy, we would observe heavy bomber missions as they passed over us and into enemy territory.

The German 88mm AA gun was a very versatile and lethal weapon. They used them as antiaircraft guns, long-range ground-target artillery, and sometimes as direct fire flat trajectory weapons against tanks and infantry. Because of this, there were always hundreds of these guns behind their frontline positions. Our planes could not fly over our front lines without drawing fire from these potent weapons.

We would watch the formations as they approached enemy territory. When the first wave of bombers was directly over us, little puffs of black smoke would appear all around the planes as these guns challenged their intrusion. The sky would look like a polka-dot quilt with bomber formations painted on it.

As soon as the black puffs began to appear, the planes in each group would move closer together to present a smaller, though a more concentrated target, and to give themselves more concentrated firepower against enemy fighters that would be diving on them as soon as they were out of the range of these guns. They would get so close that their wing tips would almost touch.

We always knew when one of them had received a disabling hit. The wounded "bird" would move away from the others lest its fire and explosion would endanger the others.

When we saw a plane move away from its group, we began to look for parachutes. We knew how many men were aboard each plane, and we would count the chutes, one by one, until all aboard were accounted for. I can tell you this, there were too many times when we did not see enough parachutes.

Occasionally, an 88mm AA shell would apparently hit a plane directly in its bomb bay, because there would be a bright flash, and in an instant the plane would no longer be there. Then, a few seconds later, you might see a wing tumbling crazily toward the earth, and a portion of the tail section descending in a spiral, but no parachutes.

Each bomber group was made up of five bombers, and we would watch the planes return from their missions, again flying through a black polka-dot sky. We would take note of the number in each group as they returned. Seldom did a group still contain the number that they started with. Following the main body of planes would come the crippled ones, each one alone and desperately trying to stay aloft a little longer as they too ran the polka-dot gauntlet again.

I will forever recall the night raids. We would hear the planes as they approached from the south, but we could not see them. By the time they were overhead, the enemy searchlights would appear, bright, narrow fingers of light reaching miles into the night sky. There would be dozens of light fingers dancing crazily across the night sky, all sweeping back and forth in an unsynchronized crisscrossing of fingers, as each light swept across the sky in every direction trying to find the invaders. It would not be long before one of the fingers struck a plane. When a light swept across a plane, its reflection returned a bright flash for all to see. After passing over the plane, this finger would immediately return to the plane and hold it steadily in its blinding light. Then all the other fingers would converge on that area of the sky, and one by one, our planes would be caught and exposed in these many fingers of lights from which they could not escape.

Then came the 88mm AA, and what were black puffs of smoke in daylight were now bright flashing lights like hundreds of fireflies on a warm summer night. Again, the planes would come together in tight formation and continue on their course, with the damaged ones breaking away from the others. At night it was not possible to count all the parachutes. We could only see the ones that happened to pass through one of the fingers of light as it descended into enemy hands.

I would be very remiss if I failed to mention the pilots of the smaller planes, the P-51s, P-38s, and P-47s. These planes were used in a variety of roles, from escorting the bombers to protect them from enemy fighters to dive bombing and strafing enemy supply lines and direct support to the ground forces. While the larger, more cumbersome heavy bombers relied largely on providence for survival, these smaller plane pilots relied mostly on their skill and daring to survive, especially when engaged with enemy fighters.

More times than I can remember, these brave, daring men have come to our aid, diving in low against intense enemy return fire to take out tanks and guns that were giving us a bad time.

We owe a lot to those brave men. Because of their successful missions, the skies were eventually almost entirely rid of enemy planes, thus making it safer for us doggies on the ground. Thank you all!

Brothers Meet, Head to Head

In other stories I have mentioned that my brother, Frank, was also on Anzio Beachhead. This story is about how we met the day after his division came onto the beachhead.

Frank was in Company F, 168th Infantry Regiment, Thirty-fourth Infantry Division. The Thirty-fourth Division was slugging it out with the Germans at the Casino Front when we landed at Anzio on January 22, 1944. In early March, the Thirty-fourth Division was pulled off the Casino Front in preparation to being committed to Anzio Beachhead.

The division actually began moving onto the beachhead March 22, 1944. About midmorning, March 23, I was sitting cross-legged in my dugout writing a letter to my parents when Frank made his unexpected appearance.

The following information in italics is not critical to this story. It is included for the purpose of helping one understand the setting in which it occurred:

My battalion was in what we called breakthrough positions at the time. Breakthrough positions are defensive positions that are a thousand or so yards behind the most forward frontline positions. They are called breakthrough positions because they are intended to intercept and stop an enemy attack if they should break through our frontlines. In these positions one can be a little relaxed and even get out of one's hole for brief periods without being picked off by a sniper or machine gun. Time in breakthrough positions was rotated among units to give some relief from the more trying frontline duty.

Had I been in the frontline positions, Frank would not have been able to join me in daylight.

I refer to my position as a dugout, not a foxhole. We were dug in along a creek bed that was from ten to fifteen feet wide and eight to ten feet deep. My machine gun was in a conventional surface position cut into the creek bank facing the enemy. To provide protection from the elements, and from overhead shell bursts, when not actually manning the machine gun, I had excavated another hole horizontally into the creek bank near the machine gun. The top of this excavation was about three feet below the ground surface, and the bottom of the excavation was about three feet above the creek bed. You might call it a mini-cave that was just high enough to accommodate a sitting position.

In the heavy rainy season the creek could run nearly full. At the time of this incident, there was only a small amount of water in a sub-channel about one or two feet in depth. A person could walk on either side of the sub-channel to avoid the water.

As stated above, I was in my dugout writing a letter when a helmeted head appeared in front of me. I glanced up and saw what I thought was a familiar face. But the head moved on. Suddenly, I realized that the face I had just seen was Frank's. I lunged forward to poke my head out to call to him. At the same time, Frank realized that the face in the dugout was mine. He returned immediately and was in the process of poking his head in the dugout at the same time I was poking my head out.

Our helmets banged together, and the momentum of my lunge sent Frank reeling backward. He landed in a sitting position in the middle of the streambed. He just sat there for a few seconds looking up at me. Finally he said, "That's a hell of a way to greet your brother when you haven't seen him for six months."

We visited there in my dugout for an hour or so. He told me that he had been given a three-day pass to visit me. I suggested that I also try to get a pass so that we could go back near the beach for a couple of days.

I went to Sergeant Pringle with my proposal. He sent us back to our company command post so that I could petition the company commander. My request was granted, and Frank and I began our trek toward the beach.

We had not gone far before we drew a barrage of eight or ten artillery shells that were quite close. We had to dive for cover in a nearby ditch where we waited for a few minutes before hurrying on our way.

By mid-afternoon we reached the R & R center in a pine forest that was very close to the sea. We presented our passes to the officer in charge. The officer turned us over to the first sergeant who assigned us to a tent.

The next two days were spent on the beach and in the Mediterranean Sea. We talked about all the fun times we had growing up together. We especially reminisced over the many family outings on the shore of the Gulf of Mexico.

Those two days went by too fast. Frank's three days were up, but I still had a day remaining. We decided that I would go with him to his company that was in a staging area waiting to be assigned to frontline positions. We had the crazy idea of one of us being transferred to the other's company so that we could be together. We put the idea to

Frank's company commander who put the brakes on that idea immediately.

He pointed out that we would both be so concerned about the survival of the other that it would increase the danger for both of us. Also, he was sure that it would reduce our efficiency as soldiers. He would not release Frank, nor would he accept me as a transfer. We realized that he was right and thanked him for his wisdom.

I spent that night with Frank and most of the next day. I wanted to return to my unit after darkness so that I would not draw enemy fire as Frank and I had done when leaving my positions. We said our goodbyes, and I headed back "home." Those were the best four days of the war for me.

Easter service 1944 at the R & R area we referred to simply as "The Pines". (courtesy of dogfacesoldiers.org)

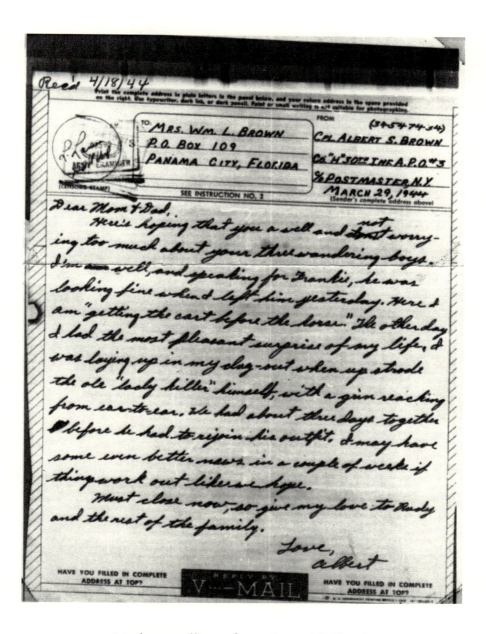

My letter telling of my time with Frank

Frankie, Albert Brown Meet On Anzio Beachhead

Private Frankie Brown, 21, and Corporal Albert Brown, 20, sons of Mr. and Mrs. William H. Brown of this city, who both have been stationed in Italy since October 1942, met for the first time recently on the Anzio beachhead where Albert is stationed, according to a letter to his parents.

Part of the letter follows: "The other day I had the most pleasant surprise of my life. I was lying in my dugout when up strode the "Lady Killer" himself with a grin from ear to ear."

The two young Panama City boys spent three days together before Frankie had to rejoin his unit. They both were sent overseas about a week apart and have been in Italy but hadn't seen each other since leaving the States, according to Mrs. Brown.

Mr. and Mrs. Brown have another son, Ensign Beverly Brown, who has been overseas a year and is now stationed in the South Pacific with the U. S. Navy on a sub chaser.

The above article appeared in the Panama City News Herald April 1944.

Two Beady Eyes

On Anzio Beachhead it was common to build a roof over a portion of our foxholes to protect us from artillery aerial bursts. We used anything we could scrounge up to provide support for the sandbag roof.

In one hole that I was in, my partner, Chester Borowski, and I made use of some steel barbed wire support posts that our engineers left behind after putting up barbed wire in front of our positions.

These posts were made from three-fourths-inch steel bars. The bottom portion was bent like a corkscrew, and the upper portion had full circle bends at one-foot intervals through which the barbed wire would pass. By placing a rod through one of the circles, the corkscrew bottom portion could be screwed into the ground so that the post stood upright.

We placed the posts flat across the portion of the hole we wanted covered. We then placed brush over the posts to bridge the spaces between the steel posts. When our sandbags were placed on top of the corkscrew portions of the posts, a tubular air space was formed beneath the bags. You could also describe them as little dark tunnels running back under the sandbags along the perimeter of the foxhole.

After we had been living in this hole for some time, Chester was selected to go on a three-day R & R. This left me alone in our little home.

The morning after Chester left, I awoke to see a pair of eyes like tiny flashlights staring at me from one of the tunnels at the far end of the hole. I tried to remember what we had been told of venomous snakes at our orientation lecture when we first arrived in Italy. I drew a blank. I could not remember anything about snakes.

I dreaded the thought of spending the day with such a visitor. It would be suicide to abandon the hole in daylight. The enemy was so close that both sides could hear each other talking.

I thought of shooting the creature, but my rifle was directly beneath the two eyes and too far for me to reach without moving. I was afraid that any movement might cause the thing to attack.

I considered my options. If I moved, I might cause the snake to strike. If I waited, it could come slithering down my rifle.

I decided that I preferred my rifle be between me and my visitor than to have my visitor between me and my rifle. I had to make a move to get the rifle.

When I lunged for the rifle, a three-inch long mouse leaped past me and was out of the hole in an instant.

A Very Special Memory

Dusk, Anzio Beachhead, Italy, May 22, 1944—the Third Infantry Division was moving out of a dense forest near the beach. The division had moved to this area from its frontline positions to prepare for what was simply referred to as the Breakout.

Tonight, the division was moving forward to the frontline. Tomorrow morning, at first light, it would spearhead the Breakout. I was one of those soldiers.

As I came out of the cover of the forest, the first thing I saw was some two-dozen Red Cross Angels lining both sides of the road. They were passing out hot chocolate and doughnuts and kissing every soldier as he passed.

Next, about two hundred yards up the road, our Third Division band was playing the Third's own tune, "The Dogface Soldier." The band was so loud that the enemy, looking down from the hills that surrounded the beachhead, was surely hearing every note. The Germans were well acquainted with The Third Division. The Third had battled them in North Africa, Sicily, and now Italy. They knew that the Blue and White Devils, as they called the division, were coming.

Still another quarter of a mile up the road was a Scottish bagpipe band. It, too, was playing "The Dogface Soldier" and blending beautifully with the Third Division band, whose notes were still audible and ringing in our ears.

We were very accustomed to having our own band send us off to battle, but this was the first time that our band had been joined by bagpipers. There is something about bagpipes that reaches deep inside you. I will never outlive the memory of that inspirational send off.

My Worst Day

My most traumatic experience involved my brother, who was also on Anzio Beachhead. He was Frank H. Brown, Company F, 168th Infantry, 34th Infantry Division.

My unit, Thirtieth Infantry, was to spearhead the attack to breakout from the beachhead and begin the drive for Rome. The attack was scheduled to begin shortly after daylight on the twenty-third. We moved up under cover of darkness the night of May 22, arriving at the frontline positions after midnight on the twenty-third.

My brother's division was holding the defensive line, and we were scheduled to move through their positions to reach our line of departure to begin our attack. Knowing that we were mingling with men of the 168th Infantry, I asked a soldier what company of the 168th was in these positions. He responded that it was Company F, my brother's company. I asked the soldier if he knew my brother and he said yes and told me that he thought Frank's foxhole was some distance to our left.

I went from hole to hole, searching for Frank that morning but to no avail. He obviously was not in the area that I had been told. I searched in other areas but no Frank. When it began to show light in the east, I had to give up my search and join my people for the upcoming attack.

Company G, Thirtieth, was to lead the assault. My machine-gun platoon was assigned to support Company G. I had been recently promoted to liaison corporal. As liaison, it was my duty to stay with the commanding officer of the attacking company. My primary responsibility was to help him find opportunities for our guns to aid in the attack and to drop back and guide the guns forward to selected positions when they were needed.

At first light, our artillery and mortars began the bombardment of the German positions in preparation for the coming assault. In response to our preparations, the Germans responded with their guns, one of them was an 88mm antiaircraft gun, which they frequently used on ground targets. This gun had been so placed that it was firing right up the dry creek bed along which many of the Thirty-fourth Division soldiers were entrenched and which we were using to reach our line of departure.

As we were moving along the creek bed, we were caught in the murderous fire of this 88mm, along with the 168th Regiment soldiers. By the time the German 88mm was silenced, Company G was so decimated that it could not mount an attack. Company F, Thirtieth, was assigned to lead the attack in Company G's place. My machine guns and I were reassigned to support Company F.

Moving through the creek bed, it was difficult to avoid stepping on the dead and wounded of the 168th and Thirtieth regiments. All the while, I was still looking for my brother, hoping I would not find him here. As they say, after infantry soldiers have been in the lines for a time, they all look alike. In any event, my eyes fell on this mortally wounded soldier wearing the Thirty-Fourth Division insignia. To my horror, it was Frank. I dropped my rifle and knelt beside him and held him close for a few seconds and then offered him a drink from my canteen.

As he opened his mouth to accept the drink, my eyes met his, close up. It was then that I realized I had made a mistake. It was not my brother after all. I cannot describe what I felt nor can I explain why I reacted the way I did, but I withdrew my canteen without giving the soldier the drink I had offered. I will forever be haunted by the puzzled look in that soldier's eyes as I withdrew the offer. How many times have I wished that I had given him that drink?

Recovering from this shock, I picked up my rifle and hurried to join Company F just in time for the scheduled assault. We charged forward some thirty to forty yards when I saw the flashes of an enemy machine gun. I dropped to one knee and prepared to fire in the direction of the flashes. Before I could fire, I was hurled into the air by an exploding shell that landed within a yard or two of me.

In a millisecond, as I felt the full force of the explosion pushing me into the air, I had the thought that this was the end for me. It was strange, but my mind accepted that fate calmly and matter-of-factly.

I was unconscious for a short time. Company F had advanced about a hundred yards by the time I recovered. My helmet was gone. I had been hurled ten feet or more. I have no idea how far my helmet might have gone. In any event, it was nowhere to be seen. I laid claim to the helmet of another soldier who no longer had need of one and hurried to catch up with the others.

As I was catching up, I realized that I was not hearing the shells that were exploding everywhere. There were flashes from rifles and machine guns but no sound, only a loud roaring in my ears, similar to the sound one gets from holding a seashell to one's ear.

By midmorning we had taken our first objective and were preparing for a possible counterattack. This was my first chance to check myself for damages. I had more than twenty holes in my clothing and equipment. Nearly half of my canteen was missing. I had two pebbles imbedded in my right cheek. A silver identification bracelet that my sister Trudy had sent me fell to the ground when I pulled up my shirtsleeve. A shell fragment had passed through my sleeve and had taken about an inch of the chain with it. Examination of my cartridge belt disclosed that a thick whetstone that I carried in one of the back pockets had stopped a shell fragment. The whetstone was broken, but it had stopped the shell fragment that otherwise would have entered my right kidney. By some miracle I was not really damaged physically. But I had lost my hearing.

After several hours, hearing returned to my left ear. And finally, hearing returned to the right ear the following morning. Those few hours on the battlefield without my hearing were the most frightening of all. A battlefield is definitely a place where all senses are in critical need.

A few weeks later I received a letter from Frank and learned that he had gone to the hospital with an illness and was not with his company that day.

Let it be known that Frank survived the war and lived a full life until November 1987, when he died from serious blood circulatory problems. I never told him of the incident that I have just related.

My Comrades and Me

The above bracelet was sent to me from my sister, Trudy, while I was in Anzio Beachhead. She also sent one to Frank. Note that the engraver got our serial numbers mixed up. My serial number was 94547434. (See my dog tags.) Frank' serial number was 94547419, which is on his bracelet with my name. Our numbers were so close together because we were inducted together.

The bracelet was cut off my arm during the breakout from Anzio Beachhead May 23, 1944. A mortar shell exploded about three feet from me, hurling me several feet. The shell fragments put more than twenty holes through my clothing. One fragment took part of this bracelet with it. The portion of the chain that is missing is no doubt buried in some Italian vineyard now.

The bracelet was not lost because it was held to my arm by the sleeve of the long john undershirt I was wearing. I discovered the broken bracelet while counting the holes in my clothing and equipment.

My Brother

Dawn breaks! Cannons roar! Soldiers die!
Anzio Beachhead—Breakout! "Charge!" was the cry.
Lying among the dead and dying
Was my brother Frank. There was no denying.

His wounds were grave. His breaths were few.
In shock! I stood and wondered what to do.
In his eyes I saw the pain and fear.
Taking him in my arms, I held him near.

Perhaps a drink of water would ease the pain.
As my canteen touched his lips our eyes met, up close, again.
It was then I saw that this was not my brother.
Oh dear Lord, what he needed was his mother.

Stunned, I brought the canteen down and took the drink away.
And then, the look he gave me will forever in me stay.
I have no understanding as to why I did this terrible thing.
If I could explain it, perhaps some comfort it would bring.

**So I left him there dying in the sand.
The truth of it I failed to understand.
But now the truth I see. Though he had a different mother,
The man I held that day really was my brother.**

Al Brown

Written on May 23, 2010, the sixty-sixth anniversary of the Breakout, following four months of hell on Anzio Beachhead, Italy.

First Lieutenant Eric W. Tatlock

In prior episodes I have referred to Capt. James H. Greene as our company commander. While on Anzio Beachhead Captain Greene was transferred to the command of Company G. Lieutenant Tatlock was given command of Company H, my company.

The position of company commander called for the rank of captain. Lieutenant Tatlock was killed before his advancement was approved.

He had been our company executive officer under Captain Greene. We all knew him well and had great respect for him. His first concern was always the well-being of his men. He was always finding ways to make our situation better. It was this trait that led to his being killed.

After two days of bitter fighting, May 23 and 24, 1944, the German's beachhead defenses were broken. The enemy began to drop back to other defensive positions. Bridges had been destroyed to delay our pursuit.

My battalion, the Second Battalion, had been the spearhead battalion for the Thirtieth Regiment on May 23 and 24. On the morning of May 25, the Second Battalion moved to regimental reserve as the First Battalion took up the attack and began a drive on the town of Cori.

The bridge over a deep ravine on the road to Cori had been destroyed. Our engineers were quick to put up a footbridge for the infantry, but it would take a day or two to complete a structure that would support vehicles. In the meantime, vehicles of every type were backed up for a mile or more.

The Second Battalion, now in reserve, was moving up to follow the First Battalion across the ravine and on toward Cori. As our march was beginning, Lieutenant Tatlock pulled up beside us in his jeep with a trailer behind it. He said that we had a long walk ahead of us to reach the ravine. He instructed us to put our equipment in his trailer, and he would take it as far the ravine.

The machine-gun tripod weighed fifty-one pounds, the gun weighed forty-seven pounds, and each ammo bearer carried forty pounds of ammunition. Being pretty tired from two days of fighting, we welcomed this relief. Lieutenant Tatlock had his driver stay close behind us as we made the three—or four-mile march to the ravine.

When we were nearing the ravine, Lieutenant Tatlock pulled up beside us and announced that he would pull ahead and get as close to the ravine as possible. We could pick up our equipment as we passed his jeep. He had his driver pull onto the shoulder very near the front of the line of waiting vehicles.

About that time, three of our P51 fighter planes appeared overhead. The P51, while designed as a fighter plane, was also used extensively as a dive-bomber. It was equipped to carry two five-hundred-pound bombs under its wings.

At first, the planes were a welcome sight. A lot of the men on the ground waved to them.

My thought was that our First Battalion, in its advance on Cori, had called them in for support. After all, they would not have tank or close artillery support until the bridge was completed.

I continued to watch the planes. They had dropped to a lower elevation and were now flying parallel to our column. They were about a quarter mile to our right. Suddenly, the lead plane dipped its left wing and made a ninety-degree left turn and began a dive toward the head of our column. The other two planes followed the first plane, and all three were now diving toward us.

I watched in disbelief as the first plane released its two 500-pound bombs. I watched the bombs as they arched toward the ground. I was thankful, as the bombs landed a safe distance short of our column. I then turned my eyes to the second plane and watched its bombs land a safe distance beyond the intended target. Then I saw the third plane release its bombs. I did not like what I saw. It appeared that its bombs were on a trajectory that would be very close to its target.

Unfortunately, I was right. My last sight of Lieutenant Tatlock and his driver was as they were attempting to climb the back slope of the roadway ditch. The bombs hit between them and the jeep. There was not much left of them for the grave registration team to pick up.

Next, I heard someone shout a warning. I looked to the left and saw the planes coming straight at us. Smoke was puffing from their wings as their wing-mounted machine guns were strafing us. I was directly in front of the lead plane. I hit the ground and held my breath as bullets kicked up dirt all around me.

The planes were circling for a third pass, when the radio operator on one of our tanks contacted them and called them off.

If Lieutenant Tatlock had had less compassion for his men, he would not have been where he was when those bombs landed. Who can say that he and his driver would not have survived the war?

It was not easy to see our commanding officer killed, especially when he died making our lives a little easier.

The bombs destroyed all of our machine guns and much of the ammunition. We were issued replacements the next morning.

Lieutenant Tatlock—Epilogue

Being attacked by our own planes happened occasionally. I had been involved in such attacks before. But in every case, it was the fault of the troops on the ground. When being eyed by planes, friend or foe, it is necessary to remain calm and continue walking as though you have no fear. The logic is this: All soldiers are trained in the recognition of aircraft. Even if the plane is so high that you cannot make out its markings, it is easily identifiable by its shape.

The converse is not true for the pilot looking down on the heads of men walking along a highway or moving across a field. Differences in uniforms are not distinguishable to him. The pilot relies heavily upon how the troops respond to his presence. The pilot has every right to assume that the people on the ground are able to identify him as friend or foe. A sure way to provoke an attack is for the ground troops to scatter and run for cover. This is true regardless of the planes' identity.

In every other incident of attack by our own aircraft that I experienced, it was triggered by ground troops running for cover. Most of the time everyone followed orders to hold position and would not run, but occasionally, a new replacement from the States would panic and run in spite of orders to the contrary. This in turn would cause others to break and run. Invariably this would bring the planes in on you.

However, the attack that killed Lieutenant Tatlock and his driver was totally inexcusable. Consider the following facts:

1) The column of vehicles was backed up on the Allies' side of the ravine. Any idiot should know that the Germans are not going to destroy a bridge *before* its army crosses it. The vehicles would have to be Allied vehicles.
2) Every vehicle or piece of equipment carried identifying symbols that were designed to be recognized from the air. American vehicles were all marked with large white stars. British vehicles were all marked with their symbol of concentric circles similar to a bull's-eye target. Some of the vehicles were ambulances marked with large white squares and red crosses in the center. None of the vehicles were marked with black crosses, as would have been the case if they were German.
3) Everyone on the ground behaved appropriately. Everyone held position and continued walking. Many made friendly gestures and waved to the planes.

It was obvious that neither of these pilots had enough basic intelligence to be trusted with an airplane.

Their stupidity and lack of training is further evidenced by the fact that they attacked at ninety degrees to the long axis of their target. Everyone (or so I thought) knows that the most effective way to attack a target is in line with its longer axis. In attacking via the long axis, the range is unimportant. All bombs and bullets will strike somewhere within the long axis limits. Alignment with the target is not a problem. It is visual.

Had the three planes attacked in line with the highway, the two bombs that fell short and the two bombs that overshot the highway would have landed somewhere on the target that was more than a mile in length. Also, all of their strafing bullets would have hit somewhere on the target area.

While sheer stupidity was the cause of the attack, it was that same stupidity that kept it from being ten times the disaster that it was.

The attackers' squadron was identified from the markings on the planes. They were from a squadron that has received much acclaim for their exploits during the war. I have seen several television programs lauding their activities.

I could divulge their identity here, but I will not. It would serve no useful purpose now and would only reflect badly on the entire squadron. I am sure that most of their pilots are deserving of the praises they have received. I would not want the actions of these three to bring down the reputations of the good pilots.

Soon after this attack, the army and army air corps (as the air force was then known) came to an agreement that yellow smoke would be a signal that the troops on the ground were allies. We were never without a few yellow smoke grenades. This signal worked quite well for us.

Negligent, Lost, and Lucky

Dreams! Some people say they never dream. I dream almost every time I fall asleep. For many years after the war, the majority of my dreams were spawned from my war experiences. In recent years I have pretty much gotten over the war-related, dreams and now my dreams run the gambit of whatever the subconscious can imagine. However, there is still a war-related dream that comes back occasionally in different forms.

This dream is spawned by an experience I had on June 2, 1944, during my battalion's drive on Cave, Italy, a small village about ten miles north of Valmontone. The battalion's mission was to clear enemy from the area between Valmontone and Cave and to protect the division's right rear from a surprise attack.

My platoon was assigned in support of Company G, commanded by Capt. Hugh E. Wardlaw. At this time, I held the rank of corporal, and I was the liaison between the rifle company and my machine-gun platoon. My primary responsibility was to move with the headquarters personnel of the company we were supporting and to be available to its commanding officer when our machine guns were needed. Normal procedure was for the CO to give me general directions as to the fields of fire for the guns. I was then to reconnoiter the area and choose specific gun positions. While I looked for gun positions, Pfc. Chester F. Borowski, my runner, would go back and guide the platoon to the forward positions.

In the late afternoon, as we were advancing toward Cave, we stopped for what turned out to be about ten minutes for reasons not shared with me. We were about to pass through a field of very tall brown grass. I recall that it stood some seven or eight feet high. It was obviously intended to become hay at harvest time, which would be soon.

About fifty yards to our left, the ground dropped away quite steeply and a crystal clear spring flowed freely from a pipe that had been driven into the bank. Seeing several soldiers filling their canteens at this spring, Chester and I decided to fill our canteens that were nearly empty.

As we waited our turn at the spring, three teenage girls came up to express their joy and appreciation for being liberated. Chester and I engaged them in conversation for a while and then filled our canteens. When we reached the higher ground where we had been, everyone was gone. Apparently the time we spent with the girls had been much longer than we realized. Following the trail of bent grass where Company G had traveled, we charged ahead as fast as we could. As we came out of the hay field, we were confronted with a real dilemma.

We were at the fork of two valleys passing on opposite sides of a hill to our front, and not a soldier was in sight. The terrain was now a combination of large brush and trees giving us very limited visibility. Did Company G go to the left or to the right of the hill? Or did it proceed straight ahead up the hill?

At this point I realized that I was in serious trouble. I had been negligent and derelict in my duties. I was not where I was supposed to be and was not able to carry out my military obligations. Since this was a combat situation, I could be tried as a deserter. The penalty for desertion in combat is execution by firing squad. I did not need to be reminded of past notices posted on our company bulletin board reporting the sentences of other Third Division soldiers, using the phrase, "to be executed at dawn by musketry." (They used the time-honored word, "musketry.")

Even if I managed to catch up before my services were needed, I could still be court-martialed for dereliction of duty, which I was clearly guilty of. A merciful sentence would be reduction to private, and the court-martial would be on my otherwise clean service record.

I had three choices: left of the hill, right of the hill, or straight ahead up the hill. I chose to take the valley to the right. After about ten minutes, moving as fast as the brush and rocky terrain permitted and without seeing any sign of Company G, I decided to move to the hill to our left. Perhaps high ground would give me a better chance to spot the other troops. It would also give me a chance to get glimpses of both valleys.

There was a foot trail along the ridgeline that I chose to follow. We had only traveled a short distance along this trail when we came upon two American soldiers who were lying in pools of blood. Their throats were cut so deeply that their heads were nearly off. There was no sign of their weapons near their bodies. This told me that they had been taken prisoner earlier. Occasionally, the enemy would execute prisoners that could slow them down when they were retreating. From this, I knew that the Germans were retreating in a hurry. The bodies were well below normal temperature but not totally cold either. I guessed that they had been dead more than a half hour but less than an hour.

Shortly after this, we met five Italian women moving toward us as fast as they could travel. One of the younger women was carrying a very old woman piggyback. As they went past us, they were obviously frightened out of their wits. They were shouting and pointing excitedly in the direction we were heading. They were telling us that the Germans were near.

To continue in that direction was very risky. But risking ambush by the enemy was still better than the certainty of the firing squad if we turned back. So we continued on but more slowly and with much more caution.

Finally, as the sun was setting and twilight was upon us, we came to the end of the ridge. Before leaving the high ground, I searched the hill to our right with my field glasses. I thought I had seen people moving about. Through the binoculars, I saw soldiers frantically digging foxholes. Refining the focus of the binoculars, I was able to determine that the helmets were American, not German.

Chester and I made the four or five hundred yards from one hill to the other in record time. I could not be more relieved when the soldiers turned out to be Company G, Thirtieth Infantry. How lucky can you be?

I reported to Captain Wardlaw immediately. He was noticeably irritated that I had not been available sooner. He had already decided on gun positions, which he pointed out to me. Since gun positions were already selected, I was free to go back to guide the platoon forward, which I did. By this time it was totally dark. I found my platoon sergeant, Jim Pringle, first. He asked, "Where have you been?" I said, "I'll tell you the details later." Jim told me that Captain Wardlaw had called our platoon leader, First Lt. Donald L. Haynes, on the radio to report that he could not find me with his headquarters personnel. Lieutenant Haynes told Jim that if I had dropped behind, he would file court-martial proceedings against me immediately.

When I found Lieutenant Haynes, he asked me, "Corporal, where have you been?" I deliberately avoided the question and said, "Sir, I have just come from Captain Wardlaw and am prepared to take you to the gun positions he has selected." Lieutenant Haynes said, "Lead on, Corporal." I moved out quickly before he could insist that I respond to his question.

Later that evening I gave my platoon sergeant, Jim Pringle, a full, detailed report of my misadventure. Jim responded that, since I had arrived in time to meet my obligations, no harm had been done. He told me that unless Lieutenant Haynes specifically asked for a report, he would say nothing. Thanks to Jim, I escaped formal punishment but did not escape a gnawing sense of guilt that I had been negligent to the possible detriment to fellow soldiers.

Since this was not something that I was proud of, I have intentionally left it out of my memoirs until now. Maybe this will help my subconscious to let it go.

A Lost Day

May 23 through June 5, 1944, was two weeks of constant fighting and pursuit of the enemy. This time period began with the Breakout from the Anzio Beachhead and culminated in the capture of a portion of Rome. Opportunities for rest or sleep were very limited. These opportunities varied from only a few minutes to a few hours. Seldom did we get more than four or five hours of sleep at one time.

By evening of June 4, we were just outside the city limits of Rome. At a late-night briefing, we were informed that Germany had declared Rome an open city. They pledged to withdraw without fighting inside the city. However, we would have to clear a sector of the city that was assigned to our regiment. Our mission was to make sure that the enemy had indeed withdrawn. This required moving on foot through all the streets in our sector, from south to north.

We began our march through Rome early the next morning, June 5. We were mobbed by wildly celebrating citizens the entire day.

We were so exhausted that we were literally walking in our sleep half of the time. Now that we felt reasonably safe, it was just natural to relax. Being relaxed, our adrenaline was pretty much turned off. Occasionally we would stop for some reason known only to those at the head of the column. Many of us would fall asleep every time we stopped and would have to be nudged awake when it was time to move again.

This continued the entire day until about 5:00 p.m. We had just cleared the north city limit and were approaching an Italian fort. We were told that we were to secure the fort and hold. Other units were going to move through us and continue the advance.

When we were maybe two hundred yards from the fort, an enemy rear guard force opened fire on us. In an instant, adrenaline kicked in, and everyone was suddenly alert and awake. However, the enemy pulled out with only a very brief firefight. I don't think either side took casualties in the exchanges. Apparently the Germans just wanted to make it official that the war was on again.

That incident demonstrated how quickly exhausted troops can be revitalized on adrenaline alone.

After making certain that there were no more enemy in the fort or lurking nearby, we were ordered to set up defenses and settle in for the night. I lay down in a sheltered spot on a concrete slab just outside one of the entrances to the fort. This was around 6:00 p.m. on June 5, 1944. I fell asleep instantly.

When I awoke, the sun was about forty-five degrees above the horizon. I judged it to be about 10:00 a.m. I smelled a very pleasant odor that went straight to my taste buds. I was as hungry as I have ever been. Investigating, I saw several Italian women gathered around an outdoor community oven that was about one hundred yards away. They were removing large round loaves of bread from the oven on long wooden paddles. I decided right then that I was going to supplement my C-Ration with some of that hot, fresh bread. I grabbed a couple of chocolate bars from my pack and a few other items and headed to the bottom of the slope to where the oven was located. I was going to do some trading.

Proceeding down the slope, I passed a group of GIs gathered around one of our tanks. They were listening to the latest news on the tank's radio. Everyone was very excited. I asked what was going on. They said that the Allies had invaded France at a place called Normandy.

I asked for more details and was told that some of our troops were already several miles in from the landing site. I was puzzled by that information. The landings had taken place about daylight. Now it was about 10:00 a.m., only four or five hours after daylight. How could they be several miles inland so soon?

I remarked that that was incredible progress in only four or five hours. One of the men responded that the landings had taken place the day before. I wondered aloud, "Why hadn't we heard something about the landings while we were moving through Rome yesterday?"

One of the men responded that it was the day before yesterday that we had moved through Rome.

It took some effort, but the guys finally convinced me that it was June 7. I had slept for about forty hours without stirring. I cannot say that I remember D-Day, June 6, 1944, but I will always remember where I was and what I was doing when the boys hit the beaches at Normandy.

I continued on to the oven and traded the chocolate and other items for a loaf of hot bread. The bread was a real treat that I shared with the men in my platoon.

A Plan Not Needed

The other experiences in this book are about events that really happened. This one is about an event that never happened.

At the end of our first week on Anzio Beachhead, it became obvious that we did not have the resources to break out. By the end of the second week, it became uncertain if we could still hold the beachhead.

With this uncertainty, Fifth Army Headquarters quickly devised an evacuation plan to salvage as much as possible. It was a plan that we troops in the frontline were not told of. We first learned of it four months later, after we were in Rome and taking a very welcomed breather.

The plan was to be executed only in the event that the enemy should make a major breakthrough that seriously threatened the entire beachhead.

The plan called for placing a maximum concentration of artillery and naval gunfire along a line that stretched completely across the beachhead and between the beach and the enemy. The plan would require every gun to place continuous fire on its designated zone until its entire supply of ammunition was expended. This gunfire was to be supplemented by continuous bombing and strafing by our air force along the same line. No guns would be available to support our frontline troops, who would be trapped beyond this line with the advancing enemy.

The plan hoped to provide a protective curtain to buy time for evacuating the beachhead to the maximum extent possible.

As it turned out, there were a few very serious gains made by the enemy, but all were successfully driven back before any of them reached a state that would trigger this last-ditch order. Had the order been given to execute this desperate plan, we frontline troops would have been trapped without help or supplies. We would have met the same fate as the Darby Rangers.

The Failure at Anzio

The book *Anzio*, written by Wynford Vaughan-Thomas, goes into great detail about the planning and the arguments, pro and con, by the highest-ranking American and British generals.

Wynford Vaughan-Thomas was a British war correspondent who was assigned to Fifth Army Headquarters, Italy. He, along with other correspondents, was privy to a lot of firsthand information through briefings and personal friendships with the top generals.

After the war was over, and Thomas returned to his newspaper office in London, he discovered that his secretary had diligently kept and filed away every dispatch that he had sent during the war, whether they had been used or not. His secretary urged him to use that wealth of information to write the true story of *Anzio*. In his book, Thomas puts the blame squarely on his prime minister, Winston Churchill.

Winston Churchill liked General Alexander's plan of an invasion behind the Casino Front in Italy. His inspiration was from two landings behind enemy lines by Second Battalion, Thirtieth Infantry, in Sicily that had greatly hastened the fall of Sicily. He referred to Anzio as his "cat's claw."

In the beginning, the generals at Fifth Army approved of the idea and began making plans for the invasion. Fifth Army Headquarters wanted a minimum of four divisions to be thrown in at one time. They preferred that six divisions be committed.

After the logistics of the operation were completed and the number of ships that would be needed was determined, Churchill was informed of the plan. Churchill immediately disapproved the plan on the grounds that it tied up ships that he felt would be needed for the Normandy invasion. When Churchill was through cutting ships, there were only enough to put two divisions ashore.

Fifth Army said no to Churchill's reduction in the size of the force to be landed. Several generals said that it would be a suicide mission. One of the generals said, "There will be no survivors."

Not only were there not enough ships to put an appropriate number of troops ashore, there were not enough ships to adequately supply the troops that were to go ashore. Fifth Army insisted on more ships. Finally, Churchill agreed that a few ships could be added but that the additional ships could make only one round trip to Naples for supplies, and then they had to sail for England. Our generals would not agree to the invasion if these ships were to be limited to one round trip to Naples for supplies.

When Fifth Army Headquarters would not approve Churchill's revised plan, Churchill went over their heads and persuaded President Roosevelt to order that Churchill's plan be executed. When our commander in chief gave the order, Fifth Army had no choice. The rest is history.

The initial Anzio landing force on January 22, 1944, was made up of two infantry divisions, one paratroop regiment, and four ranger battalions. This was equivalent to about three infantry divisions. Within two weeks, the Allies brought in the Forty-fifth Infantry Division and the First Armored Division, bringing the total Allied strength to the equivalence of five divisions.

German records showed that by February 16 they had two armored divisions, four infantry divisions, one motorized division, one parachute division, and a number of independent units opposing the Allies at Anzio. This was a total equivalent strength of nine divisions.

At this point, the Allied attackers became defenders and had to fight furiously to avoid being driven into the Mediterranean as Hitler had ordered.

From this information it is obvious that the Germans built up opposition to the Anzio invasion at a much faster rate than the Allies were able to. This was due to the small size of the initial landing force due to the limited number of ships available imposed on the operation by none other than Winston Churchill. Also, because of the limited number of ships, the Allies could not resupply rapidly.

If General Lucas had been "bold" and ordered us to move rapidly and deeply into enemy territory as the "armchair" critics say he should have, we would have, with absolute certainty, been surrounded by superior forces and cut off from our feeble supply line. The result would have been what several of our generals believed, and openly expressed, "there will be no survivors."

Thank you, General Lucas, for saving my life.

Churchill, in expressing his disappointment in the result, referred to the beachhead as a "stranded whale."

During the four-month period from the landing on January 22 to the breakout on May 23, there were more than thirty thousand casualties on Anzio Beachhead. There were just over ten thousand German casualties and a little more than twenty thousand Allied casualties. The twenty thousand Allied casualties were about equally split between British forces and American forces.

Southern France

First Extraction

After Anzio and the two-week drive to Rome, we had a "Roman Holiday" that was much too brief. We entered Rome on June 5, 1944, and moved to a training site on the coast about twenty miles south of Rome on June 14, 1944. There we resumed intensive training and conditioning for another amphibious assault landing. The landing actually took place on August 15, 1944, near St. Tropez, Southern France.

It was during this period that the following incident occurred. One morning, the company was assembled in preparation to move out to begin the day's training activities when the first sergeant called my name and ordered me to report to Battalion Headquarters. He explained that my personnel file indicated that I was past due for a dental checkup.

Battalion Headquarters was bivouacked in an orange grove about five hundred yards from my company's area. I walked the five hundred yards and reported to Battalion Headquarters. I was told that the dentist awaited me between the next rows of orange trees.

Passing between two trees to the place indicated, I saw a second lieutenant and a corporal. I also saw a cast-iron dental chair, a foot-powered dentist's drill, and a table with assorted dental tools and medical supplies on it. The lieutenant appeared to be very young. I was twenty at the time, and I am certain that he was no more than two or three years my senior.

I saluted the lieutenant, gave my name, and stated that I was reporting as ordered. The lieutenant returned the salute and invited me to take a seat in his nineteenth-century dental chair. The chair was very high. It required a full leap assisted by push-ups with both arms to get into it. If I had known what was about to take place over the next four hours, I would have declined the invitation and signed whatever papers would be required to relieve the US Army of any responsibility for my teeth from that day forward to eternity. It was straight up 8:00 a.m. when I took my seat, and it was noon when I made my grateful descent.

The first five or ten minutes was spent with the lieutenant checking all my teeth one by one. He then announced those happy words—"no new cavities". I was delighted that I was not going to find out how well the foot-powered drill worked. As I prepared to leap from the chair, the lieutenant added, "But you have one tooth that is being crowded out by the teeth on either side of it." He went on to say that if allowed to continue, all three teeth would be adversely affected. But if he removed the tooth that was being pushed outward by the other two, the others would then move together and close the gap. He strongly urged me to allow him to remove the tooth that was being pushed outward.

I had been brought up to trust doctors and follow their advice. So I agreed. The lieutenant picked up his tooth-pulling pliers from the table and began. The tooth to be removed was the third tooth right of center in my lower jaw.

My tormentor began pulling upward with all of his strength, almost lifting me from the chair. Then he began rocking the pliers with a twisting motion. Then it happened. With a sharp *crack*, he broke off the top half of the tooth. I noticed the lieutenant turn a little pale, and the corporal, looking on, was not smiling. I said, "You broke the tooth, didn't you, sir?" He replied, "Yes, but there is enough left so that I can still get a good grip on it." I said, "Get on with it then."

So in round two there was no change in plan, he still lifted with all his might while applying the same rocking and twisting motion as before. *Crack*! Same result. The lieutenant turned two shades whiter, and the corporal's jaw was almost touching his chest.

I stated the obvious, "Broke again." The lieutenant confirmed.

Then the lieutenant said, "I have a confession to make. I never finished dental school. I was drafted into the army while I was in my junior year." Then he added, "This is my first extraction." I responded that this was also my first extraction and that it appeared we were going to learn together.

He swabbed my gums thoroughly with alcohol and then, with a scalpel, opened my gum all the way to the base of the tooth, exposing the jawbone. Then using the foot-powered drill, with the corporal doing the work, the lieutenant began drilling a horizontal groove across the tooth. The drill was far from being the fastest spinning drill in the world. The lieutenant kept yelling at the corporal, "Faster, faster." This was between late June and early August, and it was a very hot, sunny day. We were all soaked in sweat. I was concerned that the corporal would collapse before the job was finished.

Finally, the lieutenant was satisfied with the groove and, with a chisel seated in the groove, he began pushing and lifting on the tooth with the chisel held firmly in both hands.

The chair was equipped with a concave headrest mounted on an adjustable steel rod. It was this headrest that prevented my head from being separated from the rest of me as my tormentor used all the strength he could muster. Occasionally, the chisel would slip out of the groove, and the chisel would lunge deep inside my mouth but always stopped just short of doing damage. After surviving four months on Anzio Beachhead, I could see me dying from a chisel to the brain by way of my mouth.

After ten or more minutes of this, my ingenious tormentor came up with another brilliant idea. He picked up a small, but heavy for its size, mallet and handed it to the corporal. He instructed the corporal to strike the end of the chisel with the mallet whenever he, the lieutenant, gave the command. So for several more minutes, it was, push, lift, *tap*, push, lift, "oops", *tap*.

Finally, the portion of the tooth above the groove separated from the bottom portion. My two tormentors took a well-deserved ten-minute break. When the break was over, they returned to the same procedure—drill a groove and with a chisel, lift, push, and *tap*—until, finally, the same result was achieved. This continued until the entire tooth lay on the lieutenant's table in a total of six pieces.

Then after another break, the lieutenant obtained a needle and heavy black thread from his table. He threaded the needle and then looked me in the eye with a whipped puppy look but didn't say anything. I spoke for him. I said, "I know, this is your first suture." He responded in the affirmative and promised to do the best that he could.

I told him to proceed. Whatever the result, it would be better than I could do.

Finally, as stated earlier, I dismounted from the chair and headed back to my company area at noon. All of the above took place without benefit of any type of pain relief. The lieutenant had none to administer.

Purple Onion

August 14, 1944, I was on an LCI (Landing craft, Infantry) anchored in Corsica harbor. Our craft was part of a huge armada assembling for an invasion of Southern France the next morning, August 15, 1944.

An LCI is a small ship and has cooking facilities only for the sailors. Therefore, we were given the same rations that we have when on the frontlines. This did not make us very happy.

The weather was warm and sunny, and in the midafternoon, some of us decided to go swimming. We would dive in from the ship's railing and climb back up via a rope ladder.

Now there were many ships in the convoy, and they were at anchor all around us. One of the big ships dumped its garbage overboard and the garbage began floating on the tide past our LCI. Well, much of it was not garbage to us. There were whole carrots, potatoes, heads of lettuce, and other assorted vegetables in the mix. Some of these were not rotted and were without flaws of any kind.

Well, we Doggies had a field day gathering up these prizes to go with our evening rations. I managed to retrieve a huge purple onion that I shared with the men in my machine-gun section. We chopped it up and mixed it in our cans of C-Rations. C-Rations never tasted so good.

Some of the men made a delicious soup from the assorted vegetables on their one-burner Coleman stoves.

It was a day to remember.

August 14, 1944, aboard LCI approaching Corsica harbor to rendezvous with other ships in the invasion fleet prior to August 15th invasion of Southern France.

See memoir "Purple Onion".
From camera: (1) ?, (2) Al Brown, (3) Jim Pringle, (4) ?, (5) Roland Romberger, (6) Sgt. Nash, (7) Steve ?, (8) ?. On the deck: (1) Manuel Lopez, (2) With Helmet ?, (3) ? Rivera (squinting), (4) ? Breletic (In doorwat_.

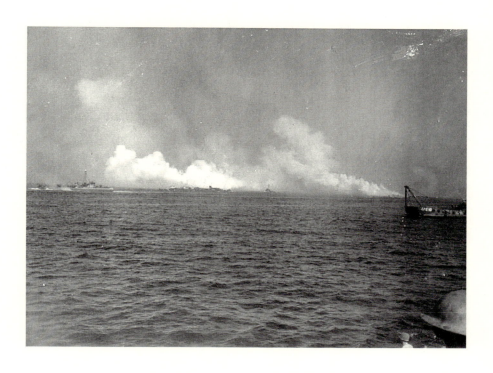

Southern France Invasion August 15, 1944. (courtesy of dogfacesoldiers.org)

Very Dull Day

What to write? Just what to say? .... Could I properly tell of the grime and the dirt;
Tell the folks what's new today? .... Of bodies that sag, yet minds alert;
Censorship often blocks the way. .... And of my soul, where I am mortally hurt?
To what's in our hearts, the answer's nay. .... There's all of this and more to say.
So, I'll report, "Nothing new-very dull day." ..... But it's, "Nothing new-very dull day."

The ruin of cities, the bestial war, ... Should I tell of shells that just miss my head;
The gaping children, weak and sore, ... Of my comrade's shirt now sticky red;
There's all of this, and even more. .... Of the ghostlike melody of singing lead?
But for lack of things to say, ... In spite of this, I'll act gay,
I'll write, "Nothing new-very dull day." .... And it's, "Nothing new-very dull day."

Would they understand of each man's toil; .... Should I write of corpses on battle's lawn;
Of our seething emotions brought to boil; .... And of the eerie quiet of the stillborn dawn;
Of American blood reddening the soil? .... And of the rotten stench when the cold is gone?
Can't really think of what to say, ... No! The proper thing to say
So it's, "Nothing new-very dull day." .... Is, "Nothing new-very dull day."

The above poem was written by a combat infantryman and published in the "Stars and Stripes" April 1945.

D-Day, Southern France

August 15, 1944, the Seventh US Army invaded Southern France a few miles East of Marseille. The Third and Forty-fifth US Divisions were spearheading the landings.

In our army, infantry soldiers were put ashore mainly in two types of landing craft. One was the LCVP. LCVP stands for Landing Craft, Vehicles, or Personnel. It would transport one jeep with trailer, or it would accommodate about forty soldiers with their equipment. The other was the Landing craft, Infantry (LCI).

The LCVP were also known as a "Higgins Boats" after the name of the company that built them. They were much smaller than the LCI and had a flat bottom so that they could normally pass through the surf and drop their ramps onto the beach. They could then reverse gears and back off the beach to return to the mother ship for more troops, jeeps, or supplies. Because they could reach the beach (hopefully) with their payloads, they were used to transport troops of the first wave. The steel plates on the bow ramp gave protection to the troops until the last instant, and then (hopefully) when the ramp was dropped, deposit them onto the beach where they could charge rapidly against enemy positions without being slowed by having to wade ashore.

The LCI was larger and had a deeper draft. Its bow would bottom out in about four or five feet of water. It had the advantage of bringing a larger force ashore (about 200-250 soldiers). It was equipped with a long ramp on each side that extended about twenty feet beyond the bow. When these ramps were dropped, the troops were deposited in waist-deep water, where they would be exposed to enemy fire while slowly wading ashore. For that reason, they normally were not used in the first wave. It was very important that a beachhead, however small, be established so that the troops wading ashore from an LCI would have a better chance.

At the Southern France landing, I was part of the second wave, and we came in on LCIs. The landings were made in the daylight. The reason for that was that our Special Services "Frogmen" had checked the waters and the beaches and had determined that the waters were heavily mined with floating antiship mines and that the beaches were heavily mined. The boat operators needed to be able to watch for the floating mines, and the troops would need to see the tripwires for the land mines. Landing in darkness would have greatly increased the risks.

I was the leader of First Section, First Platoon of Company H. Therefore I was the first man to debark via the port ramp. As I was approaching the bottom of my ramp, I saw an antiship mine bobbing up and down only inches from the ramp. It was about two feet in diameter with detonator spikes protruding in all directions. I thought, "Woe am I if that mine bumps this ramp." I moved faster than I have ever moved before and warned my men to do likewise. Fortunately it did not strike the ramp, and everyone got to the beach safely.

After getting to the beach, I began leading my men, single file, through the land mines. What I saw was large artillery shells planted in the ground with their detonator nose tips protruding from the ground. They were planted in clusters of five shells. They were in about ten-foot squares, with one shell at each corner of the square and one shell in the center. Every shell in the cluster was connected via trip wires. This included diagonal trip wires to the center shell. If any one of the wires were struck, all five shells would detonate.

I immediately saw the wisdom of the daylight landing. I very carefully located each trip wire and pointed it out to the man behind me, who, in turn, pointed it out to the man following him. Each man pointed each wire out to the man behind him. The width of the minefield was about twenty yards, and necessarily, progress was slow. It took my section about five minutes to cross this strip of mines. Thank God we were not under fire.

Fortunately for us, the fighting in the north following the Normandy invasion had drawn many of the German defenders from Southern France to oppose our forces there. As a result, the beach defenses were not fully manned. Because of that, our landing in the south was not as difficult as some of the four landings made by the Third Division during the war. Even so, it still was no "walk in the park."

As the invasion force departs Naples in mid-August under the slopes of Mt. Vesuvius, the memories of Anzio's bloody four-month stalemate for the 3rd and 45th divisions, the catastrophic crossing of the Rapido River by the 36th Division and the 45th's assault on the Gustav Line below Monte Cassino are still fresh and vivid memories. (courtesy of dogfacesoldiers.org)

At 0800 on August 15th landing ships make formation as they begin the journey to the beachhead. More than 90,000 amphibious and 9,000 airborne troops participated in the initial two-day southern France landings at three main beachheads. The slow move of the Italian thrust set the southern France landings back by two months. (National Archives) (courtesy of dogfacesoldiers.org)

LCTs on the way to Red Beach in the Bay of Cavalaire look through a naval bombardment of the beachhead. Also part of the Dragoon plan was a 322-glider air assault called Dove with Canadian, British and American troops assisting the landings around Le Muy. The call for a daylight landing was due to the defensive mining of the water and the beaches in the area. (courtesy of dogfacesoldiers.org)

A British-operated LCT turns for its run to the beach. For the Third Division, it was the fourth amphibious assault; for the 36th Div, the second; and for the 45th Div., the third. The three divisions made up the American VI Corps under Gen. Lucian K. Truscott. The entire invasion force faced 11 German Divisions in the south of France totaling about 230,000 troops. (courtesy of dogfacesoldiers.org)

Major General John W. O'Daniel takes command of the beachhead near St. Tropez. O'Daniel, appointed division commander at Anzio, led the Third Division through France, into Germany and craftily directed the division's capture of Berchtesgaden at the end of the European conflict. (courtesy of dogfacesoldiers.org)

The Third Medical Battalion is carried to shore on LCI 188. Federal Shipbuilding and Drydock in Kearny, New Jersey built this LCI(L). (courtesy of dogfacesoldiers.org)

The Third Medical Battalion tests the waters of the Mediterranean off the ramps of an LCI at Red Beach. The early LCIs had side ramps, a 25-man crew and a weight of 246 tons. (courtesy of dogfacesoldiers.org)

A taut line is held to aid the transfer of the medical troops from LCI 188. (courtesy of dogfacesoldiers.org)

This model of the LCI was designed to carry six officers and 182 enlisted men. It carried an armament of five 20-mm cannons. (courtesy of dogfacesoldiers.org)

Stop it Yourself

We invaded Southern France August 15, 1944. The German Nineteenth Army that opposed us began a withdrawal up the Rhone Valley. They wanted to pull back to the Vosges Mountains, where they would have a tremendous advantage in setting up a defensive front and would have much shorter supply lines.

The enemy was making a controlled withdrawal, something the Germans were very skilled at. They always left combat units behind to delay us, while the main body withdrew as rapidly as possible. We never knew where these delaying units would be. This required our constant probing with combat patrols to locate them before our main body was caught in their defensive traps. One night my machine-gun section was assigned to a rifle platoon on one of these combat-reconnaissance patrols.

Now I mean no disrespect toward the officer in command, but many of our officers had no more military background or training than the enlisted men. Since there was only one officer commanding a platoon of thirty to forty men, and since he was always at or near the front of his men, the casualty rate was quite high among platoon leaders; and they were constantly being replaced by officers straight from the States. Until these officers acquired a week or two of on-the-job training, we had to be very careful in following their orders.

Our patrol had been moving westerly along a two-lane paved road. When we came to a "T" intersection with another road of the same design, our column turned right onto the other road in a northerly direction. After traveling a short distance along this road, the column stopped. My machine-gun section followed immediately behind the rifle platoon. This put us at the rear of the column and still very near the intersection.

I never knew why we had stopped. I guessed that the lieutenant at the head of the column was under a blanket, referring to a map. After a wait of a few minutes I heard a *sqwueeck-sqwuack, clank, clank* about a hundred yards behind us. The sounds continued, and it was obvious the sounds were getting closer. I had recognized the sound instantly. It was a German tank changing its position and was moving very slowly in an effort to keep its noise level as low as possible.

On night patrols we communicated by whispering to the man next to us and having him pass it along via the man next to him. I sent the following message forward to the lieutenant: "Tank approaching from the rear." This message was passed forward. The lieutenant passed back the following message: "Stop it. If it is one of ours, send it forward."

Well, there were two important elements missing from the lieutenant's order: One, how were we to stop the tank with nothing heavier than a 30-caliber machine gun? Two, what should we do if it was not one of ours?

By this time, the tank was getting uncomfortably close, so I passed back the following message, "Stop it yourself. I'm getting my men off the road." Soon after moving my men a comfortable distance from the road, the lieutenant decided that my advice had merit, and he and his men joined us.

As we lay quietly off the road for a minute or two, the sounds changed into sounds that told me the tank was making a slow turning movement on a paved surface. The tank was turning right and proceeding up the road we had come from. The tank had been parked a hundred or so feet south of the intersection. We had passed right under its nose, so to speak, when we passed through the intersection. The benefits of silence on night patrols were clearly demonstrated by this experience.

We waited about ten minutes until we felt it was safe and then moved on.

An Angry Shell in Flight

I recently wrote a poem titled "Why Not Me?" In it is a line that says, "I even saw an angry shell in flight."

The other day it occurred to me that some might ask, "So what's the big deal about seeing a shell in flight?" It is in the poem because in order to see it, it had to have passed extremely close to me. In order to see an artillery or tank shell, your observation point must be almost directly in its flight path, and your eyes must already be focused on things in its path. That is the only way it will be in your field of vision long enough to register on your retina. This is especially true with high-velocity tank projectiles, as this one was.

Throughout the war I have been in the vicinity of thousands of artillery shells and only saw this one. Nor have I heard another soldier claim to have seen one. It truly is a rare phenomenon.

This incident occurred on the back side of a hill in France. As is common practice, I and my section of machine guns were following close on the heels of the rifle platoon we were supporting. The riflemen had moved up the back side of this hill and were just beginning to descend the front slope, when they were suddenly hit with tank fire from the adjacent hill.

I and my men had just reached the crest when the shells started hitting all around us. Exposed, the riflemen had no choice but to rapidly retreat to the back slope, where I and my men had already taken refuge.

The enemy tanks were on higher ground than the crest of our hill so that by barely clearing the crest of our hill, they could place fire on troops at the base of the hill, who were advancing behind us. The enemy did not need to see them to know that they would be there because reserve units were always following close behind the attacking units.

I figured that there were at least three, or maybe four, tanks because the rate of fire was faster than gunners are able to reload. Also, the width of coverage indicated that several tanks had divided the target between them, each taking a specified zone to cover. I was near the center of one of these zones, and every few seconds, a shell would come very near me, and I would see it explode near the base of the back slope. Because I was near the crest of the hill, the shells were no more than waist high as they came over me, making the prone position the only prudent one.

Behind us, coming out of a stand of trees was a platoon-size group of men headed toward us. I began to shout and wave to them to go back, but they kept coming. As another shell hit some distance in front of them, they began running toward the safety of the hill's back slope. But there was a killing zone that they would have to pass through first. Again, I tried, without success, to turn them back.

I was looking directly at the front of this group as they were entering the danger zone. At that instant, a shell traveling four times the speed of sound passed only a foot or two over my head. The vacuum behind the shell removed my helmet. The sharp crack ripped into my ear drums, and my eyes saw a reddish-brown streak thirty or forty feet long and five or six inches wide as the shell hit a few feet in front of these men. The duration of this reddish-brown streak was like a flash of lightning. The explosion took out several of the men below, just another sight burned into my memory.

A Sergeant's Revenge

The German Nineteenth Army was being driven north from the beaches of Southern France. It was their intention to make a determined stand at what was called the Belfort Gap, the entrance to the Vosges Mountains. They needed as much time as they could buy to prepare defenses and to get as much of their army through the pass as possible.

The Germans were very skilled at delaying our advances while utilizing minimum personnel and equipment. Ambush with tanks, antiaircraft half-tracks, self-propelled artillery, and snipers were their weapons of choice. Just a few of these scattered throughout an area could be very disruptive to our advance.

In the afternoon of September 17, 1944, we were advancing from the town of Lantenot toward the town of Belmont, France. The enemy was not attempting to hold ground stubbornly. He was only using delaying tactics.

Our lead troops were coming out of a stand of trees and entering a clearing. When our lead scout was some distance into the clearing, a shot rang out, and the scout went down. A sniper claimed another victim. The scout was not killed. We could see that he was trying to crawl back toward us.

His platoon medic raced out to treat him. The medic was well identified as a noncombatant. He had a Red Cross insignia on four sides of his helmet and Red Cross armbands on both arms. Also, all frontline medics wore two large pouches filled with medications and dressings, one on each hip. They resembled the pouches you see on the back of motorcycles. It was easy to identify a medic by the large bulges on both sides. Even at night, medics stood out from other soldiers by their silhouette. There is no mistaking one of our medics for a combatant. The sniper picked him off before he could reach the man he was going to help.

Then the most amazing thing happened, a second medic dashed out in spite of having just witnessed the sniper's lack of respect for the Red Cross symbol. He was also shot.

Our advance was halted, and a search for the sniper began. After about ten minutes, his hiding place was discovered. Our troops kept firing on his position to keep him pinned down while two of our men moved in close and took him prisoner. He was a sergeant.

The prisoner was brought in to the edge of the clearing. As the German stood with his hands in the air, the sergeant of the men he had shot walked up to him and, with his rifle, delivered a horizontal butt stroke that removed his ear and a portion of his face.

The prisoner was then escorted, bleeding profusely, to the rear.

About an hour later, I was wounded (see "Saved by a Chapel"). I was taken to what was called an evacuation hospital to have shrapnel removed from my leg.

At around 9:00 p.m., I was taken into a tent and placed on an operating table. On the operating table to my left was the German sniper. He was being fed blood plasma from a bag hanging above the table.

When the doctor that was going to work on me came in, I asked him how the German sergeant to my left was doing. He said that it was a fifty-fifty chance that they could save him.

I then told the doctor what had happened and how the German got his wound. The doctor put his finger on the side of my head and said, "When you see the sergeant again, tell him to aim about here. He will save us from having to use our precious blood plasma the next time".

I did not approve of our sergeant's action. I did understand his motivation. Perhaps justice was done. I just know that I would not have abused a prisoner.

Saved by a Chapel

Late in the day on September 17, 1944, near Belmont, France, I had another close call. Thanks to a beautiful black-and-gray granite chapel, I was able to escape from a very tight situation.

This day began early. At 3:40 a.m., First Battalion, Thirtieth Regiment, was committed to an attack on the town of Lantenot. Company F, Second Battalion, attacked to the southeast from Rignovelle to assist in the First Battalion's attack on Lantenot. My machine-gun section was assigned to Company F.

The enemy stayed very active throughout the day. He was making a controlled withdrawal and was never out of contact for more than a few minutes at a time. His intention was to make a determined stand a few miles to the north at what was known as the Belfort Gap, entrance to the Vosges Mountains. He was buying as much time as possible with these tactics.

Companies E and G, Second Battalion, attacked toward Belmont. Belmont is about three miles north of Lantenot. Belmont fell to Companies E and G shortly after 2:00 p.m., and Company F entered the northern part of Lantenot a few minutes later.

After clearing Lantenot, Company F was committed to an attack to the north to clear the road between Lantenot and Belmont. We met sporadic resistance as we made our move toward Belmont. By about 6:00 p.m., we had reached a point very near Belmont and were told to hold position and wait for orders.

The position selected for one of my guns was very exposed. The other was placed in a more protected location. I decided to help my men dig the hole for the more exposed position.

This gun was being placed about three feet from the end of a thick hedge approximately four feet high. The hedge was to the left of the gun, and about another eight feet to the left was a very large log. The log was parallel to the hedge and partially under it. I had left my rifle leaning against the log. It was my thought that if we had to return fire from this location, I could use the log for small-arms protection while firing through the hedge with my rifle, as I also directed the machine gun's fire.

About twenty yards behind the gun was a granite building about twenty by thirty feet. I guessed it to be a chapel of some sort, or possibly a mausoleum. To our front was an open field that was cleared all the way to a heavily tree-lined road about three hundred yards from our gun position.

I was taking a turn at digging when I heard a voice behind me. I looked around and saw a first lieutenant with his radioman. They were artillery observers and were giving coordinates to their guns for possible future use. They were sitting on the ground in full view of any enemy that might be around as though they were on a Sunday picnic. I cautioned the lieutenant that it was very risky for him and his radio to be so exposed. His reply was "It's alright, Sergeant. G-2 reported this area cleared of enemy activity." In response, I informed him that we had been in contact with the enemy only twenty minutes earlier and that I thought it very likely that we could be fired upon.

As I turned back to my digging, I thought, "What a beautiful target we make, a machine gun and an artillery observer with radio." All are very high-priority targets. The enemy could not pass up an opportunity to get all with one long burst of fire. Before I could take another shovel of dirt, it happened. The enemy opened up with a long burst from twin 31-caliber machine guns followed by four or five 40mm antiaircraft shell bursts. The first shell exploded a few feet in front of me and about three feet above ground. A piece of shrapnel from that shell caught me in the inner part of my left thigh.

I dropped into the hole and looked back over my shoulder to see if anyone else had been hit. I saw a first lieutenant and a radioman heading for the crest of the hill. The lieutenant was leading by a good three strides and pulling away. Private First Class Goble, my number 1 gunner, whose hole I was digging, was only a few feet behind. Further to my right I saw a number of GIs breaking for the crest of the hill. They were all doing what is prudent when caught in the open without foxholes for protection. I told myself, "You are the only toy left for them. You are going to get a lot of attention."

I knew from the machine-gun fire followed by aerial bursts that I was up against one of their antiaircraft half-tracks. It is armed with a 40mm cannon and two 31-caliber machine guns. The machine guns are mounted coaxially with the cannon so that they all fire on the same line. Even though designed for antiaircraft use, it was very effective against troops and lightly armored vehicles. This was their favorite weapon for delaying actions. It was mobile and had a lot of firepower. It had to be located on the tree-lined road below me. I thought that if I could spot its location, I would try answering with my machine gun.

I raised my head to take a look. My helmet was barely above ground when I received another long burst from their machine guns, followed by four or five 40mm bursts. I saw leaves flying from the hedge as the bullets sprayed through it. I tried a second peek with the same response.

It was obvious that the officer in command had his field glasses on me, and his gunner had his finger on the trigger. I now knew that I would never be able to spot them nor return their fire. I also knew that I could not last long in such a shallow hole with 40mm shells bursting a few feet above ground.

I had been hit in the left thigh and did not know the severity of the wound. I knew it was not a bad wound unless it had broken the bone. I did not think that it had. I knew that, regardless of the severity of my wound, I had no choice but to make a run for it.

I formulated my plan. I decided that I would pull my right leg up like a frog before leaping. I would raise my head one more time to provoke another burst of fire. Then when the last shell exploded, I would push off with my right leg and duck low behind the hedge. I would grab my rifle as I passed the log and, staying as low as possible, dash for the protection of the chapel.

I raised my head as planned and got the expected response. As the last shell exploded, I pushed off. They had not expected such a move and were unprepared for it. Fortunately my wound was not serious, and I had full use of both legs. By the time they could react, I already had my rifle and was headed for the chapel. This required them to adjust their aim a bit, and by the time they fired again, I was rounding the corner of the building. I saw pieces of granite flying off the building as I dove behind it.

There was a side door that I entered. Inside were a number of other GIs who had taken refuge. Had that chapel not been where it was, there is good chance that I would not be writing about it now.

Romberger's Close Call

Pfc. Roland R. Romberger A very fine soldier.
Roland and I shared many foxholes and experiences.

On March 19, 2007, I received an e-mail from Roland R. Romberger telling me of his close encounter that occurred simultaneously with my close encounter with the enemy on September 17, 1944, near a granite chapel near Belmont, France (see my memoir, "Saved by a Chapel").

Roland was number 1 gunner for one of the machine guns under my command. As stated in my memoir, I was assisting with digging a position for one of the machine guns while Roland and his assistant gunner were digging for the other gun about fifty yards from where I was.

With Roland's permission, I am reproducing his e-mail below just as I received it.

> Hi Al and Jo,
>
> I just finished reading your memoirs for the fifth time, and being with you a good bit of the time, it sure brings back memories during our good and bad times. Who can forget the chapel we used for protection after you were wounded. I don't remember that I ever told you what happened to me during those minutes when they opened fire.
>
> When the shells were exploding above us we had not dug our gun in, nor did we have time to dig a fox hole, so we ran for the back of the church, but before I made it to the rear of the chapel machine gun bullets were hitting the ground near me and I dove on top of some riflemen who had dug a fox hole about 3 ft deep next to me. Since I was the third one on top in the hole I felt I must be crushing the one on the bottom. So, in a matter of seconds, I got out and ran to the back of the chapel for protection from the shrapnel and machineguns. My brother-in-law had just sent me a smoke pipe which I carried in my shirt pocket. Somehow it fell out of my pocket when I dove on top of those men in the hole. So, after the firing stopped, I went back to see if I could find it. The men in the hole were both dead from the shells that exploded above them. My pipe was in the bottom of the hole, lying in their blood. I never picked it up, but felt sick about the men in the foxhole. Had I stayed another half minute, my life would have ended as I would have been the first to get it. I guess

I can never understand the way things happen during war time.

Wishing you happiness and God's daily blessing.

Roland

Another Close One for Roland

In frontline combat there are many close calls, but some are a bit out of the ordinary and stay with you forever. Another such event occurred about a month following the event recorded above.

As told to me by Roland:

I had another close call in the Vosges Mountains fighting. It happened late one night in mid-October 1944. I was in a crouching position when three enemy soldiers suddenly appeared above me. The leader was carrying a submachine gun. The other two were carrying two large antitank landmines each. They were obviously on a mission to mine a roadway and had lost their bearings.

I saw the leader making a move to bring his weapon to bear on me. (My parents were German immigrants, and my entire family spoke German fluently. This was very instrumental in my survival.)

Seeing the enemy's intention, I shouted in perfect German for the soldier not to shoot. This apparently caused the soldier to think I was a friend. At any rate, he hesitated just long enough for me to grab the muzzle of the machine gun and move it to one side. At this same moment, the soldier fired the weapon, putting a burst of bullets through my hand.

I ran a few steps and dove for cover and at the same time shouted for our man, who was manning one of our guns nearby, to fire. Our man opened fire without knowing what or where his target was. Of course, his fire was not a threat to the enemy, but in the dark they had no way of knowing that, so the three of them took off running at top speed, leaving four antitank mines behind.

I was returned to unit after my hand was healed several weeks later.

Saved by a Chapel—Epilogue

In 2001, my wife, Jo Ann, and I decided to take a trip to Europe to revisit the battle sites that I had participated in. We started in Italy at the Anzio Beachhead battlegrounds where I began my combat experiences. The visit at Anzio was very successful thanks in great measure to Silvano Casaldi, citizen of Nettuno. Nettuno is near Anzio and was also within the beachhead perimeter. Silvano is most knowledgeable about everything that took place during the fighting there. As our guide, he took us to many sites that I would have never found on my own. After fifty-seven years, almost everything had changed so much that I would not have recognized what I was searching for. Jo and I are very grateful and forever indebted to him.

From Anzio we took a train to the French Riviera where we rented a car for our journey up the Rhone River Valley starting at Cavalaire, France, where the division landed on August 15, 1944.

Our visit in Cavalaire was a highlight of my life. The good citizens of Cavalaire and adjoining towns combined to entertain and honor us for three days. It was a reception that Jo and I could never have imagined. We are also forever grateful to those wonderful citizens for their kindness and generosity toward us.

With that as a send-off, we headed north toward the Rhone Valley and the Third Division's trail to Strasbourg on the Rhine.

The best part of the drive up the Rhone Valley was the beauty of the countryside. Traffic was light, allowing me to relax and really enjoy the beautiful landscape, unlike my trip in 1944. We made stops at several of the towns along the way, Brignoles, Aix, Montelimar, Besancon, Lure, and finally Belmont, which is near to where I was wounded.

Prior to Belmont, our stops were of short duration because the battles along the way were mostly short lived and there was not a lot to talk about. For the most part, I would just point out to Jo Ann the position of my unit and the part it played in the liberation of each town. But now, near Belmont, was a major prize if I could but find it. The prize would be a chapel on a hillside that provided safe refuge to me in a very dire situation. (See "Saved by a Chapel.")

As told in my memoir, it was September 17, 1944. My machine gun section was assigned in support of Company F, Thirtieth Infantry. It was late in the day, and Company F was on a mission to clear the enemy from the area between Lantenot and Belmont.

Being a supporting unit, we just followed blindly behind the riflemen as they made their advances. We never had, nor needed, maps; therefore, it was difficult for me to know the exact location of this lovely chapel. But I thought that I would remember and recognize landmarks that would lead me to my prize.

Well, we searched here. We searched there. We searched everywhere. But sadly, no chapel magically loomed before us.

In desperation, I broadened our search to areas that I really did not think were even close, but I was determined.

Our broadened search took us up an ancient, unpaved, and abandoned logging trail in the midst of a forest. I knew that this was nowhere near the place I was searching for, and I was very disappointed and dejected. I concluded that the chapel had been removed and replaced by some other structure or, possibly, enlarged to a building that I did not recognize. In any event, I was ready to give up and move on when a ray of hope appeared up the trail in the distance. There was a vehicle of some sort coming toward us. Perhaps it would be a local resident who could lead us to my prize. I did allow myself just a pinch of hope.

It turned out to be a farmer on a tractor who stopped to offer help. I tried to explain to him that we were looking for a chapel. I drew the map symbol for a church on the ground, but he still did not understand. I then wrote the date "1944" on the ground, pointed to myself, and pantomimed firing a rifle. His face lit up and asked, "American soldat?" I answered yes in my poor attempt at French, but he understood. We thought that he would have a heart attack from his uncontrolled excitement. He maneuvered his tractor around our car and motioned for us to follow him.

I am sure he had that tractor going faster than it ever travelled before, but we were able to stay with him. After a distance of about two miles, he swerved off the road and stopped the tractor in an area between a couple of barns and a house. He jumped from the tractor and ran into the house.

In less than a minute the man came out of the house followed by three women. Introductions were made. This was the Petitjean family. The man was Michel; his wife, Arlette; their daughter, Virginie; and Michel's sister, Monique Laroche. We later met Michel and Arlette's daughter, Nathalie, and son, Philippe. The following year, on a longer return visit, we met Monique's husband, Roland Laroche.

After introductions, we shared wine and cheese in their kitchen. While enjoying the refreshments, we managed to convey to them our mission to find the illusive chapel. Virginie insisted that we go with her in her car to see various small structures that she thought might be our prize. To Virginie's great disappointment, none of them passed inspection. Later, when Nathalie came home from work, she insisted that we go with her to see her candidates. Sadly, they also failed inspection. By this time it was getting late, and Jo and I had decided to give up the search and move on. We wanted to reach our next destination before dark.

Before I could announce our need to depart, we were asked to stay for dinner and to spend the night with them. It was difficult for me to decline their gracious invitation, and now, in retrospect, it was rude to put my selfish desire to stay on the schedule we had rather arbitrarily set. Notwithstanding, I did decline with the excuse that we really needed to reach our next stop before dark. They pleaded with me to change my mind, but I stood firm. At that point the six of them burst simultaneously into the loudest crying I have ever heard.

Michel was the loudest of all, and tears ran down his face in a steady stream. I could not handle that. I decided right then that nothing could make me leave now. I told Jo Ann that we were staying, and she agreed. It took us awhile, but we finally calmed them down and convinced them that we would stay.

It was then the daughter explained why it meant so much to her father to have us as guests. In 1940 her father, Michel, was four years old and German soldiers took his father and uncle away to work in their slave camps. His mother and sister, Monique, were left to run the farm. The Germans took most of what they produced, leaving them barely enough to live on.

Finally, in 1944, when Michel was eight, the war swept past them as the Third Division overran that area. They huddled in the basement as the fighting took place in the street above them. When there were no more sounds of conflict, Michel ventured out of the basement to take a look. Across the street was an American soldier who motioned for him to come. He was hesitant at first. The Germans had made him wary of soldiers.

He did finally go to the soldier who gave him his first-ever chocolate bar. That was his only contact with an American soldier until I appeared that day fifty-seven years later. At that moment we found something infinitely more precious than my chapel. From that moment to this, there is a bond between us that time cannot diminish.

Petitejean courtyard, June 2001—Jo Ann on camera duty.
(L-R standing—Monique, Al, Arlette, & Michel)
(L-R front row—Nathalie, Virginie, Gypsy & Pilippe)

Third Division soldiers rest in Faucogney from their advance north to the Moselle River and Remiremont. VI Corps was now in position to advance the Seventh Army across the Moselle River. (courtesy dogfacesoldiers.org)

Author's comment: This scene is very close to the Petitjean's home and farm. See "Saved by a Chapel—Epilogue".

My Confession

Oh what a tangled web we weave,
When first we practise to deceive!
—*Sir Walter Scott*; "Marmion," canto vi, stanza 17
Scottish author and novelist (1771-1832)

If you were paying attention while reading my other memoirs, you would have noticed that after I was wounded, the shrapnel was removed in an evacuation hospital near the frontlines in France (see "A Sergeant's Revenge"), and my recovery took place in a general hospital in Italy (see "Oops!"). But there was no mention of how I got from France to Italy. Did it not seem strange that, with my usual attention to details, there was no mention of my change of hospitals?

Would you believe that I was confused? How about, "made a mistake"? (That works well for celebrities and politicians.) OK, try this: "I just left out a few details." Alright, alright, you win. I lied! I lied by omission. My sin of the past led to my sin of the present. I throw myself on your altars of mercy and ask your forgiveness.

After the shrapnel was removed at the evacuation hospital, I, and a planeload (C-47) of other patients, were flown to an airstrip near the Mediterranean in Southern France. In fact, the landing strip was within a hundred yards of the water and parallel to the beach. It was a hastily constructed, temporary landing strip.

Now it is important to know that I was fully capable of walking, but there was a rigid rule that all patients had to be moved on a litter no matter what their physical condition. So I was moved from place to place on a litter by two litter bearers. (The unions may have had a hand in this.)

After the plane rolled to a stop, we were all carried on our litters to this extremely long tent. It was about twenty feet wide and could have easily been two hundred feet long. The tent was without a floor, and our litters were just placed on the ground. The lightly wounded, such as I, were placed to the right, and the more seriously wounded were placed to the left. It was explained to us that the ones on the right would be taken to a hospital in Marseille, and those on the left would be flown to a major hospital in Italy. The one in Italy had been operational for more than a year and was large and well equipped, whereas the one in Marseille had been in operation for less than a month and was not yet developed to handle any and all medical needs as was the one in Italy. It was obvious that I would be taken to Marseille.

It was mid-afternoon when my group arrived. At about 4:00 p.m. they began taking patients from the left side of the tent to be loaded on a plane bound for Italy. Now I was in about the eighth position from the front entrance, and I observed the litter bearers bringing back three of the patients who had just been carried out. I heard the leader of the litter teams say to these men, "I am sorry for the inconvenience. There was not room for you on that plane, but you will be on the first plane tomorrow morning." The three patients were placed in the three positions nearest the entrance and diagonally across from my position.

Not long after that, another plane load from the evacuation hospital arrived, and the wounded were carried past me to the end of the line somewhere deep inside this long tent.

When this plane was completely unloaded and the litter teams were leaving the tent, the middle patient in this group of three who were to be first in line tomorrow morning, stopped one of the teams and said, "I just saw you bring my best buddy in. Would you please move me down next to him?" They obliged and moved him somewhere beyond my vision.

Well, there I was with nothing to do but think. So I began to do just that. I thought, "The first three patients on the other side are going to Italy in the morning, except there is now a missing litter in the middle. My brother, Frank, is in Italy. I would like to see my brother. What if my litter just happened to be in that vacant spot tomorrow morning?" You surely have the picture by now.

The tent was lighted by electric lights powered by gasoline generators. At about 8:00 or 9:00 p.m., almost all lights were turned off. Just a few dimmer ones were left on so one could see to move about.

Can anyone guess what I did at around 2:00 a.m. while everyone, including the orderly, was sleeping? You got it! I took up my bed and walked. I was awakened shortly after daylight as I was being carried to a plane bound for Italy.

At first, aboard the plane, I was very proud of my achievement. But then my conscience began to work on me. I had done wrong and was taking a place that was intended for someone else. Suddenly I was no longer proud of what I had done. And then, I began to wonder what would happen to me if my deception was discovered. Now "buyer's remorse" really set in. My ride to Italy was very unpleasant.

Sir Walter Scott was so right. Once you begin on that path of deception, there is no turning back. The only way is to return to the beginning and undo the deceptions, which is what I am now attempting to do. Since I was not proud of what I had done, I was reluctant to share it with others, especially not those close to me. This has been my private secret for sixty-six years.

When the doctor examined my wound at the hospital in Italy, he exclaimed, "What are you doing here!? You should be in Marseille!" I responded, "Don't ask me, sir. I just go where they carry me." He replied, "I know. This d—army never gets things right!" Yea! Was I relieved! It appeared that my deception would not be discovered. And it never was.

Post-note:

I did get to see my brother Frank while at this hospital (see memoir, "Second Reunion").

Second Reunion

My brother Frank and I managed to spend time together twice while in Europe during WWII. The first time was on Anzio Beachhead, and the second time was eighteen months later in the US Army 300th General Hospital, Naples, Italy. After being wounded in France, I connived a plane ride to Italy (see "My Confession").

Midmorning of my first day at the 300th General Hospital, I visited the Red Cross office that was located there in the hospital. With apprehension and high emotions I was going to ask them to try to locate my brother. I hoped that I would not be given tragic news. For both of us, it was a never-ending concern for the other. When we received a letter from the other, it only meant that the other was still alive as of the date on the letter.

I spoke to a Red Cross lady at one of the service desks. I told her my situation and that I wanted to locate my brother, if possible. All I could tell her was that he was in Company F, 168th Infantry Regiment, Thirty-fourth Infantry Division, and that they were fighting in northern Italy. She asked me to take a seat in a waiting area.

I did as instructed and in an unbelievable short time, less than a half hour, the lady came to me and said, "I have located your brother. He is not in the Thirty-fourth Division. He is in the Naples Replacement Depot waiting for reassignment." I was acquainted with this replacement depot. I, as did all troops arriving from the US, passed through it on my way to join the Third Division. It is where being on KP prevented me from joining the Darby Rangers. I asked if I might be able to talk to him on the phone. She replied in the affirmative and said that he was already on the line waiting for me. I cannot tell you the relief and joy this gave me.

When I began our phone conversation, the only thing Frank wanted to know was how serious was my wound or wounds. I told him that my wound was very slight and that I was fine. He replied that he did not believe me. He said that I would not be sent to this hospital from France unless my wound or wounds were very serious. I again told him that I was fine. He said, "Well, I'll know in a few minutes because they have arranged for a jeep to bring me there." The replacement depot was not far from the hospital, and Frank arrived in about twenty minutes.

When Frank saw that I was 100 percent OK, he wanted to know how I got to Italy. I just said, "You know how the army can foul things up." I was not ready to share my embarrassing secret, not even with my brother.

It was now my turn to grill him. I wanted to know what this reassignment was all about. He told me that about two weeks earlier, a very large artillery shell (probably from one of their RR guns) exploded just a few feet from him. His last recollection was feeling this unbelievable force launching him into the air. He regained consciousness sometime later at his battalion aid station.

He was sent to an evacuation hospital for evaluation. He had no visible wounds except for a lump on his head.

He must have hit his head on a rock or something when he landed. The bottom line was that he had recurring headaches at irregular intervals.

From the evacuation hospital, he was sent to the 300th General for further observation and evaluation. After a few days of observation in the general hospital he was judged unfit for further combat and was waiting for reassignment to some noncombat unit.

For me, this was the best news I had ever received. No longer would I be wondering what his status was. It was a huge relief for me.

After bringing each other up to date on things, we just hung out in the ward, had lunch, and spent a couple of hours in the hospital recreation facilities. In the cool of the evening we took a before-dinner stroll around the hospital grounds. We talked a lot about our growing-up-together times and experiences. It was a wonderful diversion from the war. After the evening meal, a jeep came to take Frank back to the replacement center.

That truly was a great day for me. My brother was apparently not seriously injured and was not going into combat again. I could now watch for letters from him, and from home, and not be afraid to open them for fear of bad news.

To: MRS. WM. L. BROWN
701 BRICKEL
MIAMI 36, FLORIDA

From: (34547434)
S/Sgt. ALBERT S. BROWN
Co. "H" 30TH INF. A.P.O. 3
c/o P.M., NEW YORK, N.Y.
9/22/44

Dear Mom & Dad,   France,

Hope everyone is well and that you have found a place to suit you by this time. I am well except for a slight wound in the left leg. I stopped a shell fragment the other day, but it has been removed and I expect to be leaving here (the hospital) before very long. That is why I am not putting the hospital address on this letter.

Last time I heard from Frankie he was doing pretty well in more than one way (if you get what I mean).

Must close now. Wanted to drop you a line to let you know that I'm alright before you got a notice from the W.D. and started worrying.

Love, Albert

My letter informing my parents of my wound

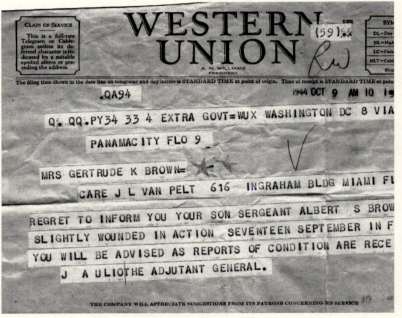

This is a copy of the telegram notifying my parents that I had been wounded. I was wounded 9/17/44 but they did not receive the notice until 10/8/44. The delay was caused by the fact that my parents had moved to Miami, as I mentioned in my memoir "Lt. James Alfred Pringle".

Oops!

In late September 1944, I was in a hospital ward recovering from surgery to remove a shell fragment from my leg.

I was assigned to the bunk that was next to a partition that divided Ward A from Ward B (see drawing below).

About three times a week, the staff would distribute a can of beer to all those who wanted it. Of course we had no way to cool the beer, so we just drank it warm.

To open the beer cans, we used a small can opener that came with our rations. The can opener had a beak-shaped blade that punctured the lid next to the rim by way of a forward rotation of the handle that it was attached to. Each forward rotation would make a cut about one quarter inch in length. After each rotation, the cutting blade had to be moved slightly to lengthen the cut with another forward rotation. By repetition, the cutter would finally make a full trip around the lid so that it could be removed.

However, for beer drinking, we only made a few cuts for an opening to drink through; and on the opposite side of the can we made a single cut for an air-breather hole.

One afternoon, my friend Errol Johnson in the adjacent bunk offered me one of his cans of beer, which I accepted. When I made the first cut with my can opener, a stream of beer shot out that would have gone at least twenty feet high if it had not hit a colonel full in the face. The colonel was coming from Ward B and entering Ward A around the partition between the two wards. His timing was very unfortunate for all involved.

The following events happened so quickly that I cannot put a timeline on them. They were so closely spaced that they were almost simultaneous. I had been sitting on the edge of my bunk when I opened the can. When the beer shot into the air, I dropped the can opener and placed my right hand over the can to stop the fountain of beer. Next, I was suddenly aware of the colonel's presence and the consequences of my actions. So I jumped to my feet and, in a panic, gave the colonel a salute with beer dripping from my right hand. I held that salute waiting for the colonel to return it while beer still overflowed from the can in my left hand.

The colonel did not return the salute but stood there staring me down while beer dripped from his chin and, after what seemed an eternity, turned and headed for the nurse's desk. I dropped my salute and decided not to report the colonel for failing to return it.

When I turned to my friend, he was trying to stuff a pillow into his mouth to stop the laughter. I then knew what had happened and what he finally admitted to. He had vigorously shaken the can of beer before offering it to me.

By the time the colonel reached the nurse's desk he had his handkerchief out and was drying his face. He called the poor nurse to attention and dressed her down one side and up the other for all to hear. He told her that there was never to be another can of beer opened inside the ward. If the patient was confined to his bunk and could not take his beer outside, it would be her responsibility to take it outside and open the can for the patient.

I felt very badly for the nurse, but it was my friend Errol Johnson's fault. He mischievously had put the chain of events into motion.

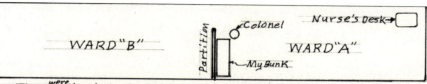

There were about forty bunks in each ward with an isle down the center.

This picture was taken outside our ward in an army hospital in Italy, September 1944.

Billy Canfield is on my right and Cecil McDonald on my left. We were classmates in Bay County High School, Panama City, Florida. We went into the service about the same time. The next time we met was in this hospital ward. Billy was in the paratroopers and Cecil was in the Thirty-fourth Infantry Division—my brother Frank's division. (We frequently ran across our friends over there. Almost all of us were in the service.)

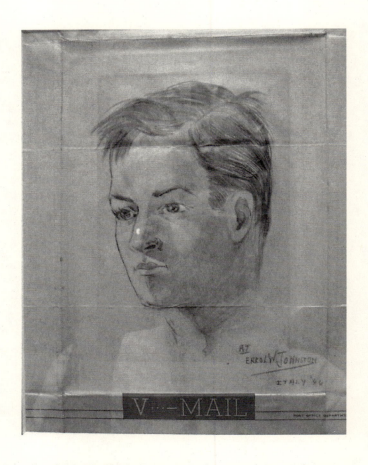

Sketch of SSG Albert S. Brown by Errol W. Johnston

Errol was assigned to the bunk next to mine while we were recovering from wounds in an army hospital in Italy, September 1944. As you can see, he used a V-mail blank form paper. His pencil was just an ordinary writing pencil. We were encouraged to use V-mail as much as possible. The V-mail would be photographed and then put on microfilm. This way they could send thousands of letters at once. The letter would be reproduced as a photo about four by six inches in size and then mailed from the US.

Colmar Pocket

Colmar Pocket, the Other Bulge

Almost everyone has heard of "The Battle of the Bulge." Few people have heard of "The Colmar Pocket." Both were very related in the German's scheme.

The "Bulge" was caused when the Germans mounted an all-out drive that broke through the Allied lines and gained a very dangerous amount of territory.

The Colmar Pocket was the result of the French First Army's inability to drive the Germans back across the Rhine River. The Seventh Army, the army my division was a part of, was to the left of the French. The French were the most southerly located army. Their zone of responsibility extended to the border of Switzerland.

Patton's Third Army was to the Seventh Army's left (north). By the end of November 1944, the Seventh Army and the Third Army had driven the enemy back across the Rhine and behind its own borders. The only enemy units west of the Rhine River in the southern region were in the vicinity of Colmar, France, in the French sector. This bulge, or pocket, extended thirty-five to forty miles west of the Rhine. This pocket posed a serious threat to the rear of the Allied armies to the north; i.e., Seventh and Third. It had to be eliminated.

Several units from the Seventh Army were sent to join the French First Army. The Third Infantry Division was one of those units to go under French command. The American divisions were to make the assault to clear the Colmar Pocket. The Third Division was the lead division in clearing this threat to the armies to the north.

At the time, the Seventh Army was just standing guard along the Rhine River. French forces took over Seventh Army positions so that the American units could be sent into the Colmar fighting.

Eliminating the Colmar Pocket began December 15, 1944, and by February 19, 1945, no more German units were west of the Rhine in the southern region.

In the beginning of this operation, the enemy was attacking aggressively in an attempt to break out and drive to the north. However, every attack was stopped cold.

The attacks in the Colmar area were coordinated with the attacks to the north that are so well-known as "The Battle of the Bulge." The German divisions from the bulge were to drive south to link up with their divisions driving north from Colmar. The object was to cut off the Third and Seventh armies along the Rhine (see map).

If the enemy had succeeded in breaking out of the Colmar Pocket, the situation could have gotten very serious indeed. Supply lines to the US Third and Seventh armies would have been cut. Patton's Third Army would have had to eliminate the threat from its rear and would not have been able to drive to the north to rescue US troops in the bulge as it did.

Holding the enemy inside the Colmar Pocket was just as critical as driving him back from the Bulge. The Third Infantry Division was at the forefront of all the Colmar fighting and was primarily responsible for stopping the enemy from breaking out as he had planned. The Third Division also took the lead in driving the enemy back and ultimately eliminating the Colmar Pocket. For these actions, the Third Division was awarded a Presidential Unit Citation.

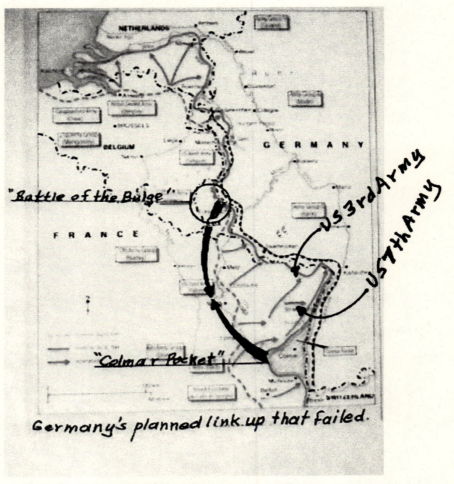

The attack in Luxemburg ("Battle of the Bulge") was code named "Northwind".
The attack out of the Colmar Pocket was code named "Southwind".

(Map copied from Google web site)

THIRD DIVISION DAILY NEWS
Public Relations office
Founded in North Africa

Austria, Vol. VII, No. 18   Sunday July 1, 1945

EXTRA! EXTRA ! EXT

PRESIDENTIAL UNIT CITATION FOR THIRD DIVISION

The Third Infantry Division, previously twice cited by the French Army, became the first American infantry division to receive the Presidential Unit Citation, it was announced by the War Department today.

The Third was honored for its fighting on the "forgotten front" of the war last winter – the Colmar Pocket campaign, called by some as bloody as the Anzio Beachhead. It joined the First Marine, the Fourth Armored and the 101st Airborne Division as the only entire divisions to be cited by the President in this war.

Destroying three entire German divisions and badly mauling another three, the Third Division spearheaded the French First Army's attack to wipe out the troublesome enemy pocket south of Strasbourg last winter while other enemy forces were continuing their abortive Ardennes push.

Counting the attached 254th Regiment and the 765th Tank Battalion, 601st Tank Destroyer Battalion and 441st AAA Battalion, a total of 21,353 officers and enlisted men are entitled to wear the Presidential Unit Badge, largest single group ever to win the award.

OFFICIAL WAR DEPARTMENT CITATION

The Third United States Infantry Division for outstanding performance in combat during the period 22 January to 6 February 1945. Fighting through heavy snow storms, across flat land raked by 88mm, 120mm mortar, artillery, tank and machinegun fire, thru enemy-infested marshes and woods, the Third Division breached the German defense wall on the northern perimeter of the Colmar Bridgehead and drove forward to isolate Colmar from the Rhine. Crossing the Fetch River from Guemar, Alsace, by stealth at 2100 hours on 22 January 1945, assault elements of the Third Division fought their way forward against mounting resistance. When the bridge constructed across the Ill River collapsed before supporting armor could arrive on the far side, two heroic battalions of the 30th Infantry Regiment held tenaciously to their small foothold across the stream against furious, tank-supported enemy attacks. Driving forward in knee-deep snow, which masked acres of densely sown mines, the men of the Third Division fought from house to house and street to street in the fortress towns of the Alsatian plain. Under furious concentrations of supporting fire, Third Division assault troops crossed the Colmar Canal in rubber boats at 2100 hours on 29 January. They drove relentlessly forward to capture six towns within eight hours, inflicting 500 casualties on the enemy during the day, and capture large quantities of booty. Troops of the Third Infantry Division slashed through to the Rhone-Rhine Canal, cutting off the garrison at Colmar and rendering the fall of the city inevitable. Then, shifting the direction of attack, the Division moved south between the Rhone-Rhine Canal and the Rhine toward Neuf Brisach and the Brisach Bridge. Simultaneously, Neuf Brisach was attacked from the west side of the Rhone-Rhine Canal and the walls scaled by ladder and by these maneuvers the fortress was captured. In one of the hardest fought and bloodiest campaigns of the war, the Third Division annihilated three enemy divisions, mauled three more, captured over 4,000 prisoners and inflicted a total of approximately 7,500 casualties on the enemy.

The Night before Christmas, 1944

Sixty-four years ago tonight, on December 24, 1944, my machine guns were in the basement of a farmhouse on the outskirts of Sigolsheim, France. The guns were positioned to fire through ground-level basement windows.

It was brutally cold and a time to be indoors whenever possible. The temperature outside was below zero with more than a foot of snow. We were told that temperatures were at a fifty-year low for that area. Our machine guns, being water cooled, required the use of antifreeze to keep the water from freezing. We were out of antifreeze, so we had filled our guns with schnapps from a barrel in the basement to tide us over until new supplies arrived.

Above us, on the second floor, leaning against the sill of an open window, was a German soldier, frozen stiff. He was still holding his rifle pointing in the direction from which we had attacked earlier that day. He was older than the average frontline soldier. I guessed him to be forty-five to fifty years old. He was wearing military-issue, wire-frame glasses with circular lenses. On his finger was a wedding band. He was obviously a husband and, in all probability, a father. He would never share another Christmas with his family. How sad.

For the most part, frontline positions were quiet. There was an occasional short machine-gun burst from one side or the other and random, harassing artillery shells could be heard intermittently, but none of this was in our immediate area. Then suddenly, at around 10:00 p.m., there was an intense incoming artillery barrage in front of our position. It lasted only a minute or two, and then it was over. A reconnaissance patrol from one of our rifle companies had been detected as it was returning from its mission, and the enemy was really giving it to them.

A couple minutes later, the patrol entered our basement carrying a badly wounded soldier and left him with us. There was nothing anyone could do for him. His brains were protruding through a shrapnel hole in the center of his forehead. I guessed the hole to be an inch and a half square. There was no exit hole. The shrapnel was still inside his skull.

I reported the wounded man to our command post and asked for a medical evacuation team. The litter bearers did not arrive until just before dawn, Christmas Day. In the meantime, the man just lay there motionless, except for light breathing. I found it difficult to believe that he was able to live with such a horrible wound. Mercifully he was not conscious.

So this was my Christmas Eve 1944—a dead enemy above me and a dying fellow soldier at my feet. While my men slept around me, I had no desire to sleep. I just sat in a chair, wondering if there was something I could and should do for this man. But nothing came to mind. It must have been about 2:00 a.m. when I could no longer see signs of breathing. He had made it to his last Christmas. One thing for certain, I knew that I would never have another Christmas Eve without this night coming back to me. I was so right.

Beginning December 23, the 15th Regiment launched attacks against Bennwihr and Sigolsheim. Bennwihr, seen here in the aftermath of the Colmar action, is nestled against the Vosges on the western edge of the Alsace plain. Bennwihr was assaulted by 139 soldiers of the regiment's I Company who faced 400 German defenders. The village was secured on Christmas Day although the fighting in the area raged into the evening. In Germany, Goebbels called it the worst Christmas of the war. (courtesy dogfacesoldiers.org)

Rude Awakening

It was about January 27 or 28, 1945, during the fighting for the town of Holtzwhir, France, when I had the following experience:

The Germans had constructed numerous concrete bunkers in this area. Some were not designed for firing weapons from. They were more suited for storing material. As we approached one of those bunkers, I decided to make sure the bunker was clear of enemy soldiers. The bunker was a hundred or more feet long and about ten or twelve feet wide.

It had entrances at each end. About five feet inside each entrance was a concrete wall in front of the opening that went more than halfway across the width of the bunker. This wall was designed to stop projectiles or shrapnel from entering the bunker. Not wanting to expose myself to possible enemy fire, and staying behind this wall, I reached around the wall and fired my rifle into the bunker. Almost immediately, there was a banging and clanging of what sounded like someone stampeding through a lot of pots and pans.

I waited a few seconds before looking around the wall. When I did, I saw two German soldiers in the far entranceway. They were obviously extremely frightened and uncertain as to what to do. I had apparently awakened them from a sound sleep. I ordered them to go outside.

As they exited their end, I moved outside and covered them with my rifle and ordered them to come to me, which they did.

When I disarmed them, one of the weapons was a knife of very high quality steel. It is hollow ground and will hold a very sharp edge. This knife is now in my wife's kitchen and is one of her favorite knives.

German knife and sheath taken from a German prisoner Holtzwhir, France, January 1945

The Other Murphy

Almost everyone in the US has heard of Audie L. Murphy, famous war hero who earned every medal for valor that our country has to offer. Audie was in Company B, Fifteenth Infantry Regiment, Third Infantry Division.

It was near Holtzwihr, France, on January 26, 1945, that Audie earned the Congressional Medal of Honor, our country's highest honor.

Three days prior to that, on January 23, and within a mile of the place where Audie earned the CMH, another Murphy willingly gave his life in order for about twenty of his comrades to live. For his sacrifice, Sgt. Jack H. Murphy, Company H, Thirtieth Infantry Regiment, Third Infantry Division, was awarded posthumously, The Distinguished Service Cross, our country's second highest award for bravery.

The following is Sgt. Jack Murphy's story.

Sergeant Murphy was squad leader of one of the two squads in my section. He was in command of one 30-caliber machine gun and seven men.

Late in the day on January 23, 1945, the Thirtieth Regiment was advancing without tank support toward

Riedwihr and Holtzwihr, France. We had no tanks because the bridge across the Ill River had collapsed when our first tank attempted to cross. We crossed on a footbridge that our engineers had built. Our lead elements were about a mile beyond the Ill River at this time.

The French First Armored Division was to attack out of Illhausern at daybreak on the twenty-third but, by late in the afternoon, still had not begun its attack.

The First and Third battalions, Thirtieth Regiment, were leading the attack. The Second Battalion (our battalion) was in reserve and following close behind the First and Third.

Knowing about the bridge collapse, the enemy sent several tanks against the infantry. He need not fear opposition from our tanks. This forced portions of the First and Third battalions to fall back rapidly. The Second Battalion was ordered to set up defenses along the banks of a smaller river named L'orchbach on our maps. The Orchbach was about two hundred yards beyond the Ill River, where the bridge had collapsed. The Orchbach Bridge was not damaged and was very capable of supporting tanks.

My people and I had just crossed the Orchbach when the word was sent back to defend there. Sergeant Murphy and his squad set up positions at the bridge. I took the second squad and set up position about eighty yards to the north. There was no time to dig in. I chose a large bomb crater for the second gun's position. The bomb crater was about eight feet in diameter and was only a few feet from the bank of L'orchbach. Our guns would be useless against the tanks. But if their infantry accompanied the tanks, our guns could be useful.

They had barely set up the machine gun when our troops came into view. They were coming out of a stand of trees about four hundred yards to our front. The enemy tanks were in close pursuit. Knowing that our 30-caliber weapons were useless against the oncoming tanks, Sergeant Murphy ordered his men to withdraw while he took over the machine gun. Murphy's number 1 gunner, Pvt. Clifton Weaver, refused to leave and stayed on to help operate the gun.

As our troops were attempting to escape the withering fire from the German tanks, a group of about twenty men took refuge in the roadside ditch about fifty yards in front of Murphy's position. As one of the tanks approached this group of men, it kept them pinned down with its machine gun. It was obvious that the intention was to hold the men there until the tank was close enough to depress its cannon and eliminate them at point-blank range.

Realizing the plight of these men, Sergeant Murphy opened fire on the tank to take its attention from the men in the ditch. The tank switched its fire to Murphy and Weaver. The duel that followed was short-lived. After a few exchanges with its machine gun, the tank ended it with one round from its cannon. However, while Murphy was dueling the tank, the trapped men were able to escape.

Murphy and Weaver knew that they could not survive such an exchange with a tank. They willingly gave their lives so that others could survive. Pvt. Clifton Weaver was awarded the Silver Star Medal posthumously for his part in that engagement.

In all, I lost five of my men at the bridge. Three of Murphy's men attempted to swim the river rather than be exposed by crossing over the bridge. These men drowned in the ice-filled river. I did not mention it before, but the temperature was around minus fifteen degrees Fahrenheit, and the ground was covered with about two feet of snow.

(Borrowed with appreciation and respect from History of Third Infantry Division in World War II.)

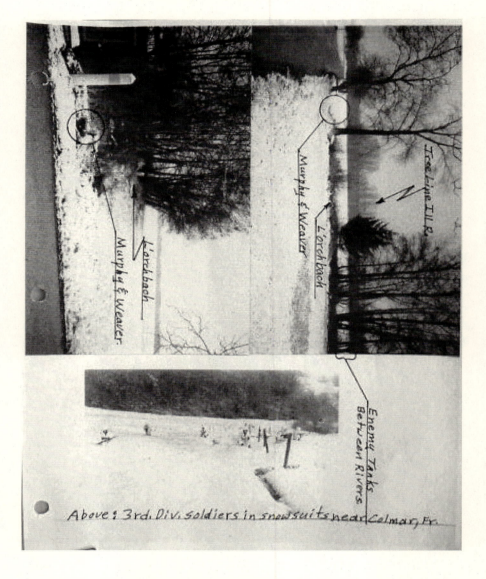

These pictures show location of Murphy's MG position and locations of the Ill & l'orchbach Rivers.

A Dash in the Snow

Late in the day on January 23, 1945, the Thirtieth Regiment was advancing without tank support toward Riedwihr and Holtzwihr, France. We had no tanks because the bridge across the Ill River had collapsed when our first tank attempted to cross. We crossed on a footbridge that our engineers had built. Our lead elements were about a mile beyond the Ill River at this time.

The French First Armored Division was to attack out of Illhausern at daybreak on the twenty-third but, by late in the afternoon, still had not begun its attack.

The First and Third battalions, Thirtieth Regiment, were leading the attack. The Second Battalion (our battalion) was in reserve and following close behind the First and Third.

Knowing about the bridge collapse, the enemy sent several tanks against the infantry. He need not fear opposition from our tanks. This forced portions of the First and Third battalions to fall back rapidly. The Second Battalion was ordered to set up defenses along the banks of a smaller river named L'orchbach on our maps. The Orchbach was about two hundred yards beyond the Ill River, where the bridge had collapsed. The Orchbach Bridge was not damaged and was very capable of supporting tanks.

My people and I had just crossed the Orchbach when the word was sent back to defend there. Sergeant Murphy and his squad set up positions at the bridge. I took the second squad and set up position about eighty yards to the north. There was no time to dig in. I chose a large bomb crater for the second gun's position. The bomb crater was about eight feet in diameter and was only a few feet from the bank of L'orchbach.

The crater was not large enough for the entire squad. The men would be without protection on top of the snow and with a river full of ice to their backs. Their rifle fire would be useless against the tanks. I had them leave their ammunition for the machine gun and instructed them to follow the stream to Illhausern, a small town to the north that was under Allied control. Two of the men and I stayed with the gun. Our machine gun would also be useless against the tanks. But if enemy infantry accompanied their tanks, our gun could be useful.

(The above six paragraphs are copied from my WWII experience entitled "The Other Murphy." The following events occurred simultaneously with and immediately after Murphy and Weaver's heroics.)

Between the bomb crater and Murphy's position was a 57mm antitank gun with a two-man crew. They were partially hidden in a clump of small trees growing along the bank of the river. This gun belonged to one of the two lead battalions and had been placed in position prior to the collapse of the Ill River Bridge.

We had barely gotten our guns set up when our troops began falling back from a stand of trees four hundred yards to our front. Soon I saw three enemy tanks pursuing them. The tanks were about two hundred yards behind and firing their machine guns. Our boys were taking casualties.

The 57mm gun to my right fired on one of the tanks. The shot was not effective. And about ten seconds later, our 57mm was history. The tank had returned the fire and knocked the gun out with one shot.

Shortly after this, I heard our machine gun at the bridge firing. Their position was not visible to me because of the small trees growing along the bank of the stream. I saw the lead tank firing its machine gun in that direction. It was obvious that Murphy and his men had just bought into some big trouble. After a few exchanges with its machine gun, the tank fired its cannon. I heard the shell impact near the bridge. After that, there was no more firing from the bridge site.

Some of the men who had been flushed from the trees fled to the north toward Illhausern. Others fled along the road past Murphy's position and crossed the Ill River using the footbridge. Some hid in small depressions in the snow in the field in front of our position. All of our troops were wearing white snowsuits that made it difficult to be seen in the snow if they did not move.

Two of the tanks crossed the Orchbach in pursuit of the men headed for the footbridge. This put them between the Ill and Orchbach Rivers and behind our position in the bomb crater. My men and I laid low in the crater. We would have no chance if spotted.

It was dusk when all of this activity began. Within a half hour it was quite dark. It was my intention to withdraw to Illhausern. But first I had to check on my men at the bridge. Now that it was dark I would have a chance to check on them without being seen. I slipped out of the bomb crater and, staying below the riverbank as much as possible, made my way to the bridge. As I passed the 57mm antitank gun, I saw that both crewmembers had been killed, and the gun was lying on one side.

When I reached the bridge position, I saw that both Murphy and Weaver were dead, and their machine gun was destroyed. I did not see any of the other members of the first squad. I learned later from two of the men that Murphy had ordered them to withdraw. They had withdrawn to Guemer. They told me that three of the men attempted to swim the river rather than risk exposure on the bridge. They were never seen again.

I returned to the bomb crater to join the two men who I had kept with me. Just as I reached the bomb crater, a tank left the road and pulled to a stop about fifty yards in front of us. Two men from the First Battalion were flushed out by the movement of this tank and joined us in the crater. I told the men that we would withdraw as soon as the tank moved away. In the meantime we had to remain motionless.

The Third Division frequently used what it called artificial moonlight to light up the battlefield at night. They would shine a number of huge searchlights into low hanging clouds, and the reflection would make it possible to see objects for short distances. The lights were on, and I was wishing that they would turn them off.

As we waited, I saw something moving on top of the snow a short distance to our left front. It turned out to be one of the First Battalion men crawling toward the tank. I could just make out that he was dragging something about four feet long. I then realized that he had a bazooka and intended to fire on the tank. In basic training we were taught that the bazooka would knock out a tank. We soon learned that it would not, but it was difficult to convince new arrivals from the States.

I knew what the outcome would be if he fired on the tank. When the soldier was about thirty feet from the tank, he stood up and shouldered the weapon. Without rising, I shouted at the man not to fire. It did no good. He fired into the right side of the tank. We watched from our crater as the tank swung its turret toward our man and cut him down with its turret-mounted machine gun. It was what we called bazooka suicide.

Apparently this activity caught the attention of one of the tanks that had crossed the Orchbach and gotten behind us. It pulled up very close to the riverbank, directly opposite our hiding place. The river was only about twenty feet wide at this point. The tank was barely ten yards from us. We could see the tank commander's head above the turret as he gave orders and looked for targets.

The riflemen who had joined us began to get edgy. I was afraid they would bolt. I grabbed them, one with each hand, and whispered to them not to move or breathe.

The tank that was in front of us moved toward the road shortly after the other tank pulled up to the river. We had traded one tank fifty yards away for one ten yards away. I was not in favor of the exchange. However, I was determined to wait it out. I felt certain that if we did not move, our white suits would save us from detection. After what seemed to be forever, but what was probably less than five minutes, the tank commander gave an order; and almost immediately the driver revved the engine. I was pleased at this. It told me that they were going to move. But the riflemen were spooked by it and leaped from the hole to run.

I heard the tank commander shout, "Auchtung Amerikaner." I ordered everyone to run for it. We stayed close to the riverbank that ran nearly ninety degrees to the left of the tank's front. In order to track us, the machine gun's aim had to be constantly changing to the left. The gunner would not be able to see his sights at night and had to rely largely on guesswork. If we had run straight away from him, his work would have been greatly simplified.

In spite of his aiming difficulties, the gunner was able to track us very well. Bullets were flying all around us. They were only missing by inches. One of the riflemen was running about ten feet in front of me. A swarm of bullets barely missed me but apparently caught the rifleman in the head. His helmet flew off, and he hit the snow in front of me. He landed like a dropped brick. One bullet spun my helmet ninety degrees on my head. I later discovered that the bullet had removed the metal connector that secured the right half of the chinstrap to the helmet.

After a dash of about eighty yards, we came to a bend in the river that put it in our path. We went feet first into the ice-filled water. We grabbed bushes above the water line and pulled ourselves up out of the water but stayed below the top of the bank.

The tank continued to sweep the area above us with machine-gun fire for another minute or two. My next concern was whether the other tank that was on our side of the river would come for us. I decided not to wait for the answer. We got out of the river and headed for Illhausern. Of the five who began the dash from the bomb crater, four made it to safety.

When we reached Illhausern, we were directed to an assembly area that had been established to reunite units that had been scattered. Outdoor gasoline heaters had been fired up to warm and dry us out. Our cooks served us hot C-Rations that warmed our insides.

Ordinance issued us new machine guns and ammunition to replace the ones left at the Orchbach.

By morning, our battalion was completely reorganized and moved out to reclaim the ground that had been lost. This time we had our tanks with us. The engineers had completed a bridge during the night.

Battle Map of the Ill River Crossing.

(Borrowed with respect and appreciation from
The History of the Third Infantry Division in WWII.)

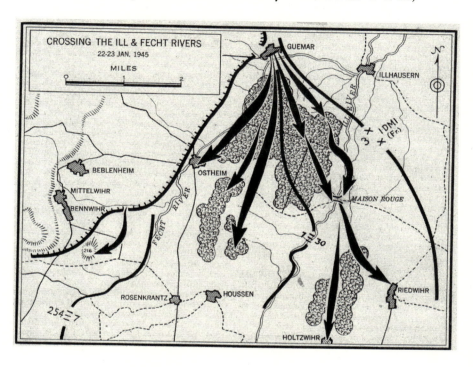

The L'orchbach is the smaller river that passes under the paved road immediately left of the letter "M" in the word Maison on the above map. The "M" also marks the place where Murphy mounted his machinegun to fire on the tanks. My position was north of Murphy's position. Tanks attacked out of Riedwihr driving First Battalion riflemen back across the Orchbach.

As you can see, the French First Armored Division's responsibility was to protect the Third Division's left flank. The 1st Armored was scheduled to begin its attack out of Illhausern in the early morning, but failed to do so. In the late afternoon when we needed them, they were not there.

The 30th Regiment advanced to the Maison Rouge Bridge where the lead tank—driven by Lt. John Harmon of C Company, 756th Tank Battalion—collapsed the standing bridge when engineers fell 15 feet short of supporting treadways. Without armor, the attacks resulted in a pull back, but through sheer will, the bridgehead at Maison Rouge was held by the Americans through the night of Jan. 23. This photo, several days later, shows a Bailey Bridge in place by Jan. 25. (courtesy dogfacesoldiers.org)

Clark's Helmet

January 28, 1945, my battalion had cleared the enemy from north of the Colmar Canal near Colmar, France. We had reached the north bank of the canal shortly after dark. We were ordered to dig in pending further orders.

Corporal Thomas L. Clark, Jr., was our platoon liaison at the time. Clark and I were going to share a foxhole this night. I wanted him with me in case I needed to communicate with the rifle company that we were then supporting.

After about two hours of digging, we had a hole that we felt was adequate, except that the fresh earth that we had thrown up from our excavation stood out in dark contrast to the two feet of snow that was on the ground. It was our intention to rest a few minutes before pulling surrounding snow over the freshly excavated earth. After all, we thought that as long as we hid our excavation before daylight, it would be OK.

We were resting with our heads above ground, trying to get acquainted with our surroundings. We were especially interested in what might be on the other bank of the canal. Suddenly, there were white flashes of a machine gun from the opposite bank of the canal. Simultaneous with the flashes, dozens of bullets were cracking within inches of our ears. Miraculously, we were not hit.

Obviously, our excavation was visible against the white snow. The canal was only about thirty feet wide, so the distance was very short. Also, our heads were easily seen at that distance.

Let me slip in a little sidebar here. The enemy machine gun fired 1,500 rounds per minute. That calculates to twenty-five rounds per second. It only needed a very short burst of fire to spray a target like a shotgun.

After a minute or two with our heads down, Clark announced that he was going to get that SOB. I told him that he would do no such thing. I pointed out that our antagonist was obviously part of a patrol that had just moved in. It was not a permanent position or they would have fired on us during the two hours that we were digging. I also knew that they would not charge our position with the canal between us. All we had to do was stay down and wait for the patrol to move on.

Clark seemed satisfied for a while, but he was not known for his patience. He wanted to take a shot at them. I tried to explain that if they were still there, the gunner would have his gun trained on our position with his finger on the trigger. Clark would never get a shot off if he tried. If they had moved on, Clark would have nothing to shoot at. So what was his point of taking the risk? I suggested that we wait an hour. Then it should be safe, and we could finish our foxhole by hiding the fresh dirt under some snow.

Clark refused to listen; he raised his head above ground, and instantly there was a burst of machine-gun fire. Clark's helmet landed on my lap. Clark's body fell back against me. My thought was that he would be dead. If he wasn't dead, I would not be able to evacuate him. Also, how could I treat head wounds in a dark foxhole?

With these thoughts racing through my mind, I ran my hands over his head and felt blood. Clark said, "Damn." Good. At least he was alive.

I examined him as best I could and determined that he had three wounds, but they were only scalp wounds. I wrapped his head with gauze from his first-aid kit. All soldiers are issued first-aid kits and are required to carry them at all times.

Clark never lost consciousness. The bandages soaked up most of the blood, and bleeding stopped in a short time.

After a good two-hour wait, he helped me pull snow over our position and then walked himself back for medical attention.

I examined his helmet. The helmet had eight holes in it, where four bullets had entered and exited. The fiberglass helmet liner, on which the steel helmet sits, had four long gashes in it. Every support strap (six) that contact the wearers head had been cut in two.

Clark told me later that he had sent the helmet and liner home for a souvenir.

Germany West of the Rhine

Lucette Libert

Lucette Libert (Li-bay)

Every time I tell myself that I am through writing memoirs, something comes up to change that resolve. Today, while going through my WWII picture album, the above picture caught my attention, naturally.

This is a picture of a French girl, whose family opened their home to us in February 1945 during a two-week break from combat. Lucette mailed this picture to my mother to keep for me. On the back is the message, "When you will be away one heart in France will wait for you." I had no idea that Lucette had such feelings nor did I know that she had sent the picture until about two months later when my mother, in a letter, wanted to know all about this charming French girl and if I planned to marry her.

Now seeing this picture with the incriminating message, I was presented with two alternatives. One, destroy the picture and all information connected with it before family members come across it and begin sending teams of investigators to France, collecting DNA samples from all natives born during November 1945 in and around Lucette's village. Or two, tell the story that I have withheld up to now.

Now this is the way it was:

After six months and four days of almost constant contact with the enemy, we were finally given a two-week breather before going back into action. The Thirtieth Regiment was assigned the area in and around the small city of Nancy, France. The Liberts lived in a small village on the outskirts of Nancy.

To give us relief from tents, our military had asked the French to open their homes to us, which most of them willingly did. I, and about half of my men, were assigned to lodge with the Liberts. They had a very large two-story home with a two-story attachment having four bedrooms and one single-story attachment with one bedroom. I and my men stayed in the two-story attachment portions of their home.

Every evening, the Liberts would invite us into their living room to visit and sip wine with them and talk (mostly pantomime) about various things. After two or three days, their daughter, Lucette, who was fourteen at the time, began to become friendly toward me. She would ask me to walk with her to the local store to pick up the day's groceries or whatever. I agreed to accompany her. She was full of energy and laughed and smiled all the time. She was very nice company, *period*. One afternoon she asked me to accompany her to the matinee at a movie house in Nancy, which I did.

About the same time Lucette began giving me attention, her parents began to ask me if I was going to come for Lucette after the war was over. This was crazy talk, and I informed them that I had no intentions of that sort toward their daughter. Lucette continued to ask me to walk to the store with her. I never refused.

When the day came that we had to leave, Lucette offered me the scarf which she is wearing in the above picture that she sent to my mother. But I refused to accept it, and Lucette seemed very hurt. So I turned to her parents for support, but they supported her and insisted that I accept the scarf. Well, I didn't want to offend a family that had been so nice to us, so I took the scarf.

A few weeks later, after the enemy had been cleared from all territory west of the Rhine, I was chosen for a three-day R & R. They were dispatching a truck to take about twenty of us to Nancy for the R & R. I decided that I would definitely pay my respects to the Liberts.

The drive to Nancy was about four hours. I was at the Liberts' front door by midafternoon. Mr. Libert came to the door and, when he saw me, shouted, "Al-bay ici" (Albert is here). Mama Libert came running, followed by a young man in his midtwenties. It was their son, whom they told us was in a German prison camp. He had been liberated and had been home a few days.

They were all excited and thought that I had come for Lucette and were talking wedding plans. I had planned to visit with them into the evening, but with these developments, I told them that I could not stay, that I was on an important mission and had to keep moving. Lucette was not home at the time, which I was grateful for. After a very short visit, I returned to Nancy and joined the others on R & R.

After returning to my unit, I told my men what had happened and how the Liberts thought I had come to marry Lucette. After having a good laugh, they confessed that they had told the Liberts that it was my intent to ask Lucette to marry me but only after the war was over. They explained that I wouldn't tell the Liberts because I might be killed and did not want to cause them grief. But if I did survive, that I would come for Lucette. Then I understood why the Liberts had asked me about my intentions toward Lucette while we were guests in their home and also why I got so much attention from Lucette.

I cannot tell you how angry this made me, and I let the guilty ones know it. They had perpertrated a cruel hoax on nice people, who had taken us in and made us feel like family. What a wonderful break it had been from the hell of war. For two weeks I felt human again. I had every intention of staying in touch with the family and possibly developing a lifetime friendship via correspondence. These men's stupidity had ended any chance of that.

Later, when my mother's letter arrived, telling about the picture Lucette had sent, I confronted them again; and they admitted that they had given the Liberts my parents' address. It would have been relatively easy to kill them.

A Close Call in Rimschweiler

Following the successful elimination of the Colmar Pocket in the French zone, the Third Division moved to the vicinity of Nancy, France, for a breather and to receive replacements and to train for the final drive into Germany. After a two-week daily training "breather," the Rock of the Marne saddled up and moved out on March 13, 1945, for the big push to end the war.

At 1:00 a.m. March 15, 1945, the Third Division crossed its line of departure; and we were on our way to Germany. The vaunted Siegfried line was dead ahead. By March 17, the Third Division reached the first fortifications of the Siegfried line.

The town of Rimschweiler was jammed right up against the main fortifications. It was a very small, compact town. At the very north end of town was a steep hill that rose a hundred feet or more to its crest. The hillside was covered with many concrete pillboxes surrounded by zigzag trenches for protection of foot soldiers.

With the town as a barrier and the steep hill behind, it was not a good location through which to launch an attack. Our main attacks would be at other locations; however, the town had to be cleared of enemy. Our commanders did not want any surprises to our flanks and rear coming out of Rimschweiler.

A combat patrol had to go in and make sure that the town was clear. My section of machine guns was selected to be a part of that patrol. We were briefed for the mission at Battalion Headquarters. Only the lieutenant, who was to lead the patrol, and sergeants that would be involved, were at the briefing. Being a staff sergeant, I was present.

We were to move out as soon as it was dark. We were to stop in the southern outskirts of Rimschweiler and wait for an artillery barrage on the northern portion of town to end before proceeding farther. They wanted to give us an advantage in case the town was occupied. We were given the name of a specific street, where we were to wait for the artillery to stop firing.

The barrage was to begin at 9:00 p.m. and was to last for twenty minutes. Only after this twenty-minute barrage were we to advance beyond the street specified. I do not now recall the name of that street, but you can bet the farm that it was burned into my brain that night.

After being satisfied that the town was clear of enemy, we were to set up defenses at the north end of town confronting the Siegfried defenses. They did not want enemy to slip back into town to disrupt the attacks that were to be launched soon.

Our patrol moved out as soon as it was dark enough. It only took about ten minutes to reach the outskirts of Rimschweiler. My section was following close behind the riflemen. I went up close to each street sign so that I could read it in the dark. I believe that the third street we came to was the street where we were to wait. But the troops in front of us kept going. I checked the time. It was about 8:30 p.m.

My first impulse was to hurry forward to catch up to the lieutenant and warn him. I then thought that the platoon leader, having radio contact with Battalion Headquarters, had probably received a message that changed the plan. Still, I felt very uneasy as we continued farther and farther into town.

Being a small town, it only took about fifteen minutes to reach the northern limits. As soon as we arrived there, I went to the lieutenant to find out where he wanted our guns placed and, more importantly, to ask about a change of plan. When I reported to him, he began to tell me where he wanted our guns placed. I interrupted him and asked if he had received a change in orders. He said no. I told him that at 9:00 p.m. we were going to receive one hell of a barrage from our artillery. He didn't know what I was talking about.

I told him that we were to wait at the street that had been specified until the barrage ended. He said that he had heard no such thing and ordered me to get my weapons in position, immediately. I told him that he could have me court-martialed tomorrow, but right then, I was getting my men out of there. That is exactly what I did.

About two minutes after my men and I reached the place where we were to wait, the lieutenant and his platoon came up the street on the double. Even as they joined us, artillery shells began to fly overhead. It was a very intense barrage. There was a continuous screaming of shells as they passed over. They were landing in the area that we had just vacated and in such rapid succession that it was difficult to distinguish one shell burst from another.

After twenty minutes of that, the guns stopped firing, and we moved back into town. The lieutenant thanked me.

For a sequel to the above, see "Stupidity in Rimschweiler."

Stupidity at Rimschweiler

The following is a sequel to "A Close Call in Rimschweiler."

My section of machine guns was part of a combat patrol into Rimschweiler on the night of March 17, 1945. Following a softening-up artillery barrage, we went through the town to the northern limits that butted up to the Siegfried line.

We had been ordered to set up defensive positions confronting the Siegfried defenses and wait for further orders.

I positioned each of the guns in basements of adjoining homes so that they could fire through the basement windows in the direction of the Siegfried defenses. I then strung telephone lines between the two positions so that I would be able to communicate with both guns no matter which house I might be in. After establishing watch schedules for both guns, I lay down for a nap.

The next morning, as soon as it was light enough to see, I moved up from the basement into the house. It was a two-story house, so I went to the second level, where I would have a better view of the hill to the north. I wanted to see the type and locations of the fortifications confronting us.

I saw several pillboxes and a lot of zigzag trenches. My immediate concern was a pillbox no more than a hundred yards away. It was so located that its field of fire was right up the space between the houses that our guns were in. The distance between the buildings was at least twenty feet. That meant it would be suicide for me to try to move from one gun to the other. I needed safe access to both gun positions.

I went downstairs to the front door. I liked what I saw. The houses on the other side of the street were staggered from the houses on my side. This meant that I could cross the street with my house protecting me from the enemy. I could then pass behind the house across the street and approach the house where the other gun was located, again, without exposure to enemy fire.

I followed this route and entered the other house via the front door and proceeded to the basement. There I warned the men of the menacing pillbox and instructed everyone that, if they wanted to visit anyone at the other gun position, they should take the route behind the house across the street. Under no circumstances was anyone to be in the space between the two houses separating our positions.

Returning to the other gun, I gave everyone there the same instructions. I then went back to the second story to study the defenses against us. After about thirty minutes, I heard machine-gun fire coming from the hillside, and I saw gun flashes coming from the pillbox directly in front of us.

I hurried to the basement to see what was going on. I was told that one of the new men (I do not recall his name) who had joined us as a replacement while we were in Nancy, had gone out a side door to go to the other gun to visit a friend he had come from the States with. He had been hit but was able to make it to the front of the other house, out of the enemy's line of fire.

I talked to my people at the other gun position by phone and asked what they knew about his condition. They reported that the man was badly wounded and that the rifle platoon's medic was tending to him. They managed to evacuate him a little while later. I do not know whether he lived or died.

That night, March 18, we were pulled out of Rimschweiler to join our battalion in the attacks against the Siegfried line beginning March 19.

Beer in Zweibrucken

My twenty-first birthday, March 20, 1945, all three regiments of the Third Division, in simultaneous attacks, breached the Siegfried line and captured its first German city, Zweibrucken.

In Germany, all civilians were to be considered potential enemies. Homes were to be searched for weapons and, of course, cleared of enemy soldiers. In the process of clearing homes in a residential neighborhood of Zweibrucken I and two of my men were checking one of the homes. On the dining room table was a pitcher of beer surrounded by several glasses just waiting to be filled. When the men saw the beer, one of them said, "Oh boy, beer." I replied, "Yes, beer waiting to kill you. Dump it out and follow me to the next house."

Without looking back, I went through the kitchen and out the back door to the next house. The two men had not caught up with me by the time I had checked the next house. I was a little concerned. I encountered other men from my section who were checking other houses in the neighborhood. I sent one of them back to find out what was delaying the men who had been with me.

About twenty minutes later, the man who went to check on the others caught up with me. He reported that he had found them rolling around on the floor in pain. He reported that he had located a man with a radio and had called for the medics to come for them. He also said that the pitcher of beer was half empty and that there were two glasses on the table with just a little beer left in them.

Those men were never returned to unit. I never knew whether they lived or died. I just chalked them up as two casualties due to insubordination and stupidity.

Germany and Austria

Bad Decision Leads to Mini Bridgehead across Rhine

I joined the Third Division on Thanksgiving Day 1943 and was assigned to First Section, First Platoon, Company H, Thirtieth Infantry Regiment. I served in the First Platoon, Company H, to the end of the war.

I arrived as a private; and by the time we were ready to cross the Rhine River the night of March 26-27, 1945, I was a staff sergeant and section leader of the First Section, First Platoon, Company H. Our primary weapons were two water-cooled, 30-caliber heavy machine guns.

Under the cover of darkness on the night of March 26, we moved up to the west bank of the Rhine River to wait for the engineers to bring up the boats that were to transport us to the east bank of the Rhine, where the Germans awaited and expected us.

The boats were brought up some time after midnight. After heavy artillery bombardment of the German positions, we were ordered to load into the boats and proceed to the east bank.

I helped the men load themselves and their equipment into one of the boats and took up a position in the bow. The engineers provided a coxswain (a corporal) to operate the outboard motor, which I think was a twenty-five-horsepower Johnson.

Our coxswain had a bit of difficulty getting the motor to start. But after a dozen pulls on the starter rope and a few choice expletives, the motor started, hesitantly for a while; and then it smoothed out to full throttle and we were on our way. However, when we were maybe one hundred yards out, the motor quit abruptly.

The coxswain began trying to restart the motor. After several fruitless pulls on the starter rope, I ordered everyone to get their shovels out and to begin paddling to the east bank.

The motor never restarted, and by the time we reached the east bank, the fast-flowing Rhine River had swept us maybe a half mile north of the scheduled landing site. I suddenly realized that I had not made the best decision when I had us paddle to the east bank. At the time I made the decision, I expected the motor would restart, and with its power, we could buck the strong current and land with the others.

Having landed so far from the main body, I fully expected that we would be annihilated or taken prisoners. By good fortune we had landed at a sheltered spot, where the bank was not too high. We tied the boat off to some heavy brush and unloaded without a sound.

Leaving the men and equipment by the boat, I crawled over the bank and explored a fan-shaped area to about fifty yards out. Not encountering the enemy, I returned to the men.

While we were still paddling across the river, the main body was already engaged with the enemy to the south of us. We could hear the shooting and see tracers flying everywhere.

Apparently, the fighting to the south had drawn the enemy troops from our landing site. Whatever the reason, I was thankful that we were not fired upon. However, I really did not expect to make our way through the two firing lines to join our troops without a fight.

The men, being burdened by the heavy equipment, would not be able to respond quickly if fired upon. It was necessary for me to be the point man. I would move ahead about fifty yards at a time, return to my unit, and bring the men to the limit of the area I had just explored. By repeating this sequence, we began moving toward the main body, where, by now, the fighting was really picking up.

I kept as close to the river bank as I could. If we were fired upon, the bank would provide a protective palisade to fight from.

Another big concern was time. It would be daylight soon, and it would be impossible to move this group of men and equipment in full daylight without detection. I moved as fast as I dared, but avoiding detection required patience and caution.

I was able to distinguish enemy machine-gun positions from ours. The Germans' tracers were white, whereas ours were pink. Of course, not all guns fired tracers, but those that did provided me a pretty good idea where the main firing lines were and the locations of the strong points. Also, it was easy to tell the difference between their machine guns and ours from the sound.

Finally, when we were maybe two hundred yards behind the enemy's main defense perimeter, I observed white tracers coming from two positions very near the river. It was obvious that we would have to break away from the comfort of the riverbank. I chose an area that seemed to have the widest space between firing positions and began moving toward it.

When I had gotten the men to within about fifty yards of the Germans' firing line, I told the men to stay put until I came for them. Even if we succeeded in slipping between the enemy strong points, we would likely be cut down by our own troops, who would logically mistake us for attacking Germans.

I found a shallow gully between two firing positions and worked my way past the Germans a few feet at a time. Divine providence was with me that morning. I reached our positions unscathed. I reported that I had sixteen men and two machine guns behind the enemy positions and that I was going back for them. I asked that they keep the enemy busy but not to fire in the direction we would be coming from.

It was truly a miracle. We succeeded in getting through to our side without a scratch and about thirty minutes before daylight.

I have often wondered what happened to that engineer corporal that I left stranded on the Germans' side of the river. I hope that he did not fall into their hands.

He probably wanted to get his hands on the stupid sergeant who paddled across the Rhine, when he could have returned to the west bank and taken another boat.

The infantry crossed the Rhine in assault boats before daylight on March 26, 1945 and established a bridgehead. By the end of the day on March 26, two bridges were completed and three divisions were on the east bank. A real tribute to our 10th Engineers.
(courtesy dogacesoldiers.org)

Anxious Moments in a Barn

One night, somewhere in Germany, my machine-gun section was following close behind the rifle company we were supporting as it advanced through a small farming village. The village had been subjected to artillery fire ahead of our advance. Many houses were ablaze. The flames stood out in contrast to the inky black night. A light rain from low hanging clouds added to our discomfort.

The riflemen in front of us were not in contact with the enemy. They were advancing cautiously in anticipation of ambush from rear guard units. From time to time, forward movement would stop as point men (scouts) would see or hear something suspicious.

It was during one of these pauses that I happened to be beside a large barn. A burning building behind me was silhouetting me. Not wanting to be a tempting target, and also to get a brief respite from the rain, I stepped into the barn. The inside of the barn was even darker than outside.

I stood just a few feet inside, with the door ajar so that I would know when the troops began to move. I had been there for less than a minute when I thought I heard someone move inside the barn. I listened intently. In a few seconds

I heard it again. It was a very faint noise, like feet moving in the straw on the floor.

I thought of how vulnerable I was in the open doorway. Anyone inside would surely see me. Was it a patriotic citizen with a pitchfork or possibly a German soldier who had fallen asleep and had failed to wake up when his comrades left? It was very common to encounter enemies similarly left behind. There was also the possibility that one of our men had decided to take five and had just awakened.

I leveled my rifle in the direction of the sound and gave a challenge. There was no response except that whoever it was began moving faster toward me. I gave a second challenge and got the same result.

When I gave my third challenge, it was in a much louder voice, and I promised to shoot. Again there was no verbal response, only faster movement toward me. By this time, whoever it was, was within pitchfork range, and I tightened my finger on the trigger. An instant before my rifle would have fired, I got a response. The farmer's cow said, "Mooooooo."

Nurnberg Medic

Nurnberg was declared by Adolph Hitler to be the most German of all German cities. It was the primary source of his political support that propelled him to power. In the center of Nurnberg was the infamous Adolph Hitler Platz, where most of his political tirades were carried out in front of many thousand cheering, fanatical followers.

Many Nurnberg citizens joined their soldiers in the fighting for Nurnberg, vowing to hold the city past Hitler's birthday as a birthday gift to him. The battle for Nurnberg began April 17, 1945. It ended on Hitler's birthday, April 20, 1945, when the Adolph Hitler Platz fell to the Second Battalion, Thirtieth Infantry.

On April 21, 1945, the Third Division held a special flag-raising ceremony in Adolph Hitler Platz, renaming it "Eiserner Michael Platz" (Iron Mike Square) in honor of the Third Division's commanding general, Major General John W. O'Daniel, who was known to his troops as Iron Mike. When the ceremony was over, a huge American flag hung atop the Zeppelinfeld in front of the Hakenkreuz (swastika), totally eclipsing it.

General Patton, commander of the Third Army, sent Iron Mike a message, asking him to preserve the Hakenkreuz that he, Patton, wanted, to have it removed and added to his personal collection of war memorabilia. The next day, Iron Mike had a demolition crew blast it into very small pieces.

The above victory did not come without its price. It came after four days of hard continuous fighting during which an incident involving a frontline medic occurred. It is that incident that I want to be the real focus of this story.

The inner city was almost totally destroyed by bombs, tanks, and artillery. The enemy made good use of basements and piles of rubble to delay our advance. Snipers were everywhere and difficult to locate in the rubble.

Just before dusk of the third day, we received fire from a sniper hidden in the rubble. The lieutenant in command ordered everyone to take cover and dispatched four men to outflank the sniper and eliminate him.

While we were waiting in an area that was out of the sniper's field of fire, I struck up a conversation with the platoon medic. He was very young, probably eighteen. His uniform was much cleaner than most of the other soldiers, and I suspected that he had not been in the frontlines very long. He told me that he had completed his training as a frontline medic a few weeks before and had just arrived from the States and was assigned to this platoon two days earlier. This was his first battle.

As we talked, we noticed one of our soldiers across the clearing that was being covered by the sniper. The soldier looked our way and went into a crouch. It was obvious that he intended to join us. Several of us motioned to him to stay put and shouted "sniper" as loud as we could.

The soldier did not heed our warning and made a dash across the open area that was about fifty yards wide. When the soldier had made it about halfway across the clearing without being fired at, I thought that maybe the sniper had left. Then with only ten yards to go, a shot rang out; I saw the soldier's body flinch as the bullet struck him. He continued to run and fell into our protected space.

The young medic was on him immediately, looking for his wound. I watched while the wound was located. The bullet had passed cleanly through the soldier's chest, from side to side, leaving two holes that were bleeding profusely. The wounded man was alive and trying to talk.

The medic rolled the man facedown and got on his knees, straddling him. Then with thick medical pads in each hand, he reached around his patient and began pressing the pads against both wounds in an effort to slow the bleeding.

Having heard the shot, the lieutenant in command came to investigate. He saw the wounded man facedown with the medic over him. The lieutenant ordered the medic to get off the man and to roll him onto his back. Without removing his hands from under the man, the medic attempted to explain to the lieutenant what he was doing. The lieutenant would not listen and again ordered that the man be placed on his back. Still, the medic resisted and tried to explain to the officer that it would be wrong to do so.

The officer shouted at the medic, "Soldier, this is a direct order. Roll that man over now." The medic reluctantly moved to one side of the soldier and rolled him over as ordered.

With the soldier on his back, the medic got two fresh pads and began holding them on the wounds. Within a minute, as all that were near looked on, the man drew his last breath and closed his eyes. The officer walked away.

The medic checked the soldier for a pulse to confirm that he was gone. He got up with moist eyes and said to me, "Sarg, I killed him." I said, "No, the war killed him. You did everything you could to save him." He then explained that he had the man facedown so that the blood would drain away from the lungs and that when he rolled him onto his back, the lungs filled with blood, drowning him.

I remember thinking, "Why isn't he blaming the lieutenant?" I wanted to blame the lieutenant but decided against it. I did tell him that he did not have to follow the lieutenant's order in that situation. The lieutenant was acting outside of his authority. That he, the medic, was the one trained in first aid, not the lieutenant.

Nurnberg was the last big battle of the war that ended May 8, 1945, eighteen days later. There were a few more skirmishes and only a few more casualties. It is a good possibility that the sniper victim was that medic's only patient in the war. I have often thought of him and wondered if he returned home feeling like a total failure.

Our frontline medics have never been given much, if any, publicity since the war. The heroics of those who got medals for killing people get a lot of publicity. We hear very little about our medics for saving people.

They did their jobs under the most difficult conditions. Often they performed first aid on the wounded in exposed places while combat troops could find cover in shell holes, ditches, and other depressions. The medic did his work wherever the wounded man happened to fall.

We always took special care of our medics. He was like a security blanket. There were many times that we would be without a medic for a few days while waiting for a replacement for one that had been killed or wounded. Moving forward without a medic gave me a naked feeling, like being without my helmet.

During the war, the War Department decided that combat infantry soldiers should be given extra hazardous duty pay and recognition. A Combat Infantryman Badge was developed. We were issued the badges and began receiving a monthly bonus of ten dollars. The frontline medics were not authorized to receive the badges or the ten-dollar bonus because they did not fight. Our hero, Bill Mauldin, did a cartoon in protest of that idiotic decision.

S/Sgt Al Brown mid-April, 1945, Germany, relaxing prior to the battle for Nurnberg.

Final Thoughts and Memories

The place was Salzburg, Austria. The date was May 7, 1945, one day before the official, unconditional German surrender in WWII on May 8. The Thirtieth Infantry Regiment had just liberated the city of Salzburg on May 5 after thirty months and ten campaigns of hard fighting that began November 8, 1942, with assault landings on North Africa. I had fought in the final seven of those ten campaigns and was watching from a second-story window of a Salzburg residence as a column of unarmed German soldiers, three abreast, marched past in the street below.

As I watched this column move past, it gradually seeped into my mind that the war was over and that I was alive. For many months my future had been limited to one minute at a time, from one shell burst to the next, from one machine-gun burst to the next; and now it was dawning on me that my future had the potential of lasting a normal life span. It was like waking from a dream and wondering whether the dream you had just experienced was real or just a dream.

As the reality took over my thinking, I experienced a euphoria that I had never experienced before or since. However, as this joy was reaching a peak, I began thinking of comrades left behind in cemeteries across Africa and

Europe, and my emotions did a 180-degree reversal until I reached a state of sadness never before experienced. I was no longer that innocent high school kid who went to war on March 12, 1943. The war had changed who I was and now am.

As I continued watching these defeated soldiers pass beneath me, I began to feel sorry for them. What must they be feeling? What would be their future in their destroyed country? Then I remembered that my mother had come from Germany and had left six brothers behind. I began to wonder if any of these men were my relatives. I wondered if somewhere among the older soldiers was one of my uncles and if among the younger ones was maybe a cousin.

Then I wondered if I had possibly, somewhere along the way, killed or seriously wounded a cousin or an uncle. Had any of these relatives nearly killed me?

With all of these thoughts racing through my mind, I fully realized the madness that war really is. And I recall a feeling of great satisfaction coming over me because we had just concluded the war to end all wars. That was the promise the politicians had made to us. Wow, how wonderful the future was going to be. Think of it, no more of this madness. How naïve that twenty-one-year-old was.

Salzburg, Austria, May 7, 1945, disarmed German soldiers as seen from the second story window of a Salzburg residence.

(Photos taken by S/Sgt. A.S. Brown as he observed the procession with mixed emotions.)

False Alarm

WWII had ended on May 8, 1945. A few days later, after we had finally convinced ourselves that we were not dreaming, that the war was really over, and we had survived, it was a time to relax. We were not concerned about tomorrow. Whatever tomorrow brought, it would not be more combat. We could handle it. Bring it on!

Then, whammo! The order came down for the Fifteenth and Thirtieth Regiments to move out with full battle gear. Intelligence reported that there were an unknown number of SS troops holding out in the mountains near Hitler's infamous Eagle's Nest. The word was that they were led by the notorious SS General Heinrich Himmler and that they were prepared to fight to the last man rather than surrender.

What a bummer! Our sense of safety was abruptly taken away. Here we go again. What a shock this was to our psyche.

So off we go into the mountains, searching for an enemy we really didn't want to find. Over a period of four or five days we swept through the area where the SS were supposed to be. No enemy troops were encountered. Finally it was decided that our commanders had received bad intelligence, and we moved back to Salzburg, where we awaited orders for occupation duty.

For once, bad intelligence was good. However, this served to remind us that we were not civilians yet but soldiers who could be ordered into danger at any time.

Why Not Me?

On my trip to hell and back
I learned that bullets, inches from your ear, do not whine, they crack!

Bombs and shells have launched me bodily.
How many times? I'm not sure, but more than three.

I have walked with comrades amid swarms of tracers in the night.
And once, in broad daylight, I even saw an angry shell in flight.

Again and again we charged the enemy lines.
We moved against bullets, shells, and mines.

We moved together, my comrades and I.
How was it determined who should live and who should die?

For years I have pondered this mystery.
Why was it them? Why not me?

Nein Heil

After the war ended, my regiment was assigned occupation duty in and around Kassell, Germany. There was a German citizen who worked with us in our search for war criminals. He was very helpful to us in identifying and locating German war criminals. This man's right arm hung to his side like the arm on a rag doll, and it was just as useless.

He was a very patriotic German, who did not agree with Hitler and the Nazi Party. He chose not to abide by the political "Heil Hitler" requirements.

One day, as part of a huge throng gathered to hear one of Hitler's tirades, he would not do the "Heil Hitler" thing along with the vast majority. His failure was observed by Gestapo agents, who watched for "enemies" of the state. He was dragged from the plaza into a building, where his right arm was secured to a table, and the Gestapo agents repeatedly smashed his arm with their rifle butts until the entire arm and hand were like jelly. He was then released and told that if he would not use his arm and hand to salute their Fuehrer, he would never use it for anything else.

At the Third Infantry Division's 91st Reunion in Arlington, Virginia, in September 2010, General Peter W. Chiarelli, Vice Chief of Staff, U. S. Army, read the following quote by Eric Severeid, World War Two news correspondent and well known radio and television news anchor.

General Chiarelli read:

"War happens inside a man. It can never be communicated. That is the tragedy and perhaps the blessing. And that is why you and your sons will be forever strangers."

Eric Severeid, CBS 1945

Special Comrades

General Lucian K. Truscott

General Truscott probably contributed more to the war effort than any other individual in our military service. This is my opinion after reading *Dogface Soldier: The Life of Lucian K. Truscott* by Wilson A. Heefner. General Truscott was everyone's everything—soldier and general. Do not challenge my opinion until after you read this excellent biography.

General Truscott was the go-to guy throughout the war and beyond whenever there was the need for innovative, efficient-minded leadership. He never failed on an assignment.

While commanding the Third Infantry Division, General Truscott set standards of training and conditioning excellence for the Third Division that made it one of the premiere divisions in the European Theater.

Recognizing that the key to stamina in combat was physical conditioning and toughness, General Truscott required everyone to be able to speed-march thirty miles in fourteen hours. To accomplish that goal, they were required to march five miles per hour the first hour, four miles per hour for the next two hours, and then maintain a pace of 3.5 miles per hour for the remaining seventeen miles. This became known as the Truscott Trot. In addition to the thirty-mile speed marches, the division did one-hour five-mile speed marches several times a week. Because of this training, the Third Division set records in Sicily, advancing through mountainous terrain with full combat loads. In one drive they advanced fifty-four miles in thirty-six hours against light enemy resistance.

General Truscott was always close to the frontline fighting, where his command decisions were made largely from firsthand observations and information. By being in touch with the fighting, he was able to make better and quicker decisions. He was truly a dogface general, who was keenly aware of the high costs being paid by his dogfaces. He always made decisions designed toward maximum efficiency and minimum casualties. His troops admired him.

We were sad to lose him as our division commander when he was moved up to command the VI Corps on Anzio Beachhead. However, we did not suffer from his loss because he named Iron Mike O'Daniel as his successor.

Iron Mike

Major General John W. O'Daniel was the best field general in the entire US Army. We dogfaces of the Third Infantry Division felt damn lucky to have him as our leader.

He was never far from the front and was often seen by frontline troops. He did not rely on others to tell him what was going on. He was there seeing it for himself. It was not uncommon for him to swoop low over his advancing troops in a Cub plane to drop a note giving instructions or to warn of the enemy's location.

The division was seldom off the lines for more than brief periods. Iron Mike always took advantage of those brief periods to address his men. It was always a formal dress parade event where he awarded medals to those who had earned them since the last parade. We would then march past the reviewing stand to the tune of "Dogface Soldier." Iron Mike would salute the first contingent of troops as they approached the reviewing stand, and he held that salute until the last soldier in the regiment was past.

There were three regiments in the division: Seventh, Fifteenth, and Thirtieth. I was in the Thirtieth. He reviewed the troops one regiment at a time. The entire division was too large to be reviewed at once.

Commander of the Thirtieth Infantry Regiment was Col. Lionel C. McGarr. In his very gravelly voice, Iron Mike began every speech to us with, "Colonel McGarr, officers and soldiers of the Thirtieth Infantry Regiment, you haven't had rest. You don't want rest. You want Glo-o-o-ory!" Then he would review our performance since our last break from the front and tell us how great we had performed and how proud he was to have such men under him.

Every speech ended exactly the same: "Soldiers, sharpen your bayonets. I'll meet you on the objective." He meant every word. He would be on the objective only minutes after it would be taken. We always knew that he was somewhere near.

General O'Daniel knew what it was like to lose a loved one in combat. He had a son in the paratroops. Private John W. O'Daniel, Jr., was killed during the Normandy invasion. He was among the first paratroopers to drop behind the beachhead.

General O'Daniel never mentioned his loss to the troops, but we all knew about it and felt his pain with him.

The last I heard of Iron Mike, he was a corps commander in Korea. They were still calling him Iron Mike.

HEADQUARTERS THIRD INFANTRY DIVISION
OFFICE OF THE COMMANDING GENERAL
APO No. 3

On this Memorial Day of 1945, the 3d Division remembers you for the contribution you have made to America and all it stands for in the loss of your loved one.

These things are hard to understand, but in a war such as this one where the gain to be had was so great and the destruction of the evil force so necessary, great sacrifice was inevitable.

We who are living know that the success of the Division, and our own very existence is due mainly to those who unselfishly gave their lives in battle. This realization will be with us always.

Now that the German Army is destroyed, you can well feel proud that through your great contribution, our nation may live as was intended: in freedom and goodness.

As Division Commander of the 3d Division, I speak from the bottom of my heart for all of us when I say be of good cheer and be ever proud that his sacrifice makes it possible for our country to be great and free forever.

[signature]

JOHN W. O'DANIEL
Major General, U. S. Army
Commanding

The above is a copy of a letter to the family of a Third Division soldier who was killed in action. Iron Mike had the letter distributed to every soldier under his command for Memorial Day 1945.

It was his way of thanking and honoring the soldiers under his command.

In debating the reasons why the Allied effort at Anzio had failed to make its objectives, 15th Army Group command passed the order through Gen. Clark's Fifth Army to change the command of VI Corps on Anzio. Third Division commander, Maj. Gen. Lucian Truscott assumed VI Corps command on Feb. 17. The Third Division command was handed to its assistant commander, Brig. Gen. John O'Daniel seen here in his command post located within mortar range of the frontline.

Lieutenant Pergament

On Anzio Beachhead one night in March, 1944, I became suddenly ill. Vomiting and diarrhea struck without warning. I was a mess. My platoon sergeant sent me back to the battalion aid station near the front. They wanted no part of me. I needed a bath and a change of clothing. They sent me to one of the hospitals farther back, near the beach.

The doctor there had me swallow two huge pills and sent me for a shower. When I got out of the shower, clean, fresh clothes were waiting for me.

I spent the rest of that night and the following day in recovery. By nightfall I was much better and ready to return to the front. I was provided with transportation back to my battalion command post. I reported to the officer in charge and told him that I was returning to my unit. The officer told me that if I hurried I could catch a jeep that was outside preparing to leave for my area of the front.

I ran outside just as the driver started the engine. I asked if I could hitch a ride. The driver replied in the affirmative. It was very dark, but I could see that there was a passenger in the front, so I jumped in the back.

On the way up I learned that they were going to our mortar positions that were a couple hundred yards behind the front. After we arrived, I asked for directions to Jim Pringles machine-gun positions. I had never been to these mortar positions before and did not know their location relative to our machine-gun positions.

One of the soldiers began to give me directions when the soldier, who was in the jeep as a passenger, cut him off. Taking over the conversation, he began to give directions that immediately told me he had no knowledge of frontline positions.

The first thing that he told me was that Pringles' guns were at Garibaldi's tomb. He then began to tell me how to get there. I knew that Garibaldi's tomb was in no-man's-land. It was constantly changing hands. Both sides wanted it for an advance-warning listening post.

I tried to tell the soldier that Pringles' guns were not at Garibaldi's tomb. I also pointed out that other parts of his information did not match the facts that I knew. He still persisted in trying to give me directions.

I finally said to him, "Look, fella, you're all wet. I'll get back without your help." The soldier became irritated and told me to go ahead and get myself killed then if I were too stubborn to listen. I told him that I would look out for me and that he should look out for himself, and I wished him luck.

On his return to battalion, I had the jeep driver drop me off at the place where we picked up rations and supplies every night. I had been on ration detail several times and knew my way from there quite well.

A few weeks later we were pulled off the lines for a breather. We were bivouacked in a pine forest near the beach. The first morning that we were there, a second lieutenant approached my platoon. We were just lounging around, enjoying the filtered sunlight streaming through the trees.

I watched him as he stopped to talk to a group of men about twenty yards from me. Some of the men appeared to be pointing to me.

The lieutenant started walking straight toward me. As I got up to meet him, I thought, "Now what have I done?" I gave him a salute that he returned.

The lieutenant opened the conversation with, "Do you remember me?" I answered that I did not. He then said, "I'm the fella that was all wet." Then I remembered the night at the mortar positions.

I apologized to the lieutenant and explained that in the darkness I did not know that he was an officer. I told him that if I had known, I would have been more respectful and that my choice of words would have been different.

He then introduced himself. He said, "I am Lt. Hyman Pergament, and I have come to tell you that you were right. I *was* all wet." Then he explained that he had just arrived from the States that night and had been briefed at the battalion command post as to the frontline situation and as to where different units of the battalion were located. He acknowledged that he didn't get as much from his briefing as he should have.

I was very impressed with an officer that could not only admit to an enlisted man that he was wrong, but one that went to so much trouble to find out my name and to look me up weeks later to apologize.

Lieutenant Pergament was assigned platoon leader of the mortar platoon of Company H the night he arrived. He remained in that capacity to the end of the war. He had a very high concern for all enlisted men and was always going out of his way to help them.

He served in a dual role as company executive officer and was responsible for censoring all of the soldiers' outgoing mail. From reading all their letters, he got to know much about each man and his personal relationships back home. He became a father figure to many of the men.

Lieutenant Pergament and I got together several times after the war. We met at several Third Division reunions and also have visited in each other's homes. Every time we met, he would remind me of our first meeting and of my insubordination. He died a few years ago. I miss him along with all the others.

Lt. James Alfred Pringle

Of all the soldiers that I was associated with during my two years of duty in Europe, Lieutenant Pringle was the most influential on me.

When I joined the Third Division in November 1943, I was assigned to his squad. He was the squad leader and held the rank of corporal at the time, even though the position called for the rank of sergeant.

Corporal Pringle was about ten years my senior. He was with the division when it landed in North Africa a year earlier on November 8, 1942. He fought in all the division's battles in North Africa, Sicily, and, up to that time, two months in Italy.

Corporal Pringle was about six feet three inches tall and spoke with a strong but soft voice. When he spoke, you listened, not because you were intimidated, but because of the respect he commanded and for the respect he had for everyone. He never gave orders. He gave instructions. He never raised his voice when directing us.

We all called him Jim. He never asked that we be formal with him. We all felt so comfortable around him it just seemed right. He was also obviously comfortable with it. Later when he became a commissioned officer, we still called him Jim, except in the most formal military situations or in the presence of other officers. The informality never interfered with his leadership. His decisions were never questioned.

Jim always put the well-being of his men above his own. At the very beginning, I knew that this was the man I wanted leading me into battle. He never disappointed me. He was my leader, my father figure, and my friend.

Corporal Pringle did not remain corporal long. As the war ground on, he was promoted to sergeant (squad leader), staff sergeant (section leader), and then tech sergeant. As tech sergeant he was given command of the platoon. After he was our platoon sergeant for a few months, he was offered what was known as a battlefield commission. But there was a catch. The army had a regulation that did not permit a soldier to be promoted from enlisted man to commissioned officer and stay with the men he had been leading. The army was concerned that because of prior friendships and informalities, the officer might have difficulty maintaining proper discipline and respect.

Jim told them that if he had to leave the men he had led for so long, they could keep the commission. He just wasn't interested. After about two weeks, they caved in and told him that they were waiving the regulation in his case and that he could stay with his platoon *and* receive the commission.

Tech Sergeant Pringle became Second Lieutenant Pringle and moved up from platoon sergeant of First Platoon to platoon leader of First Platoon. By the time the war ended, Jim was promoted to first lieutenant and became our company executive officer.

Jim was awarded the Silver Star Medal and the Bronze Star Medal, both for performances beyond and above the call of duty under enemy fire. He definitely set the example for his men. He was admired and respected by all.

Many years after the war, at a Third Division reunion, Jim brought the notebook that he kept throughout the war. In it he kept the names of every man that had been under his command. It was also a journal where he recorded the names of every man that was killed or wounded, with some comment about the circumstances of the unfortunate event.

He passed the notebook around for all to thumb through. When I had my turn with the notebook, to my surprise, the last entry was a reminder—"call Brownie." I asked him about the entry, and he told me that he had made the notation on the plane that flew him from Europe to Miami. I had been returned to the US ahead of him. His plan was to spend a day or two with me in Miami before going on to his home in Oregon. He said that he had tried to call me but that the operator told him that my parents no longer lived at that address.

When I was inducted, I was still in high school and was living with my parents in Northwest Florida. Later my parents moved to Miami and, shortly before the war ended, moved to Dade City. I had not thought to give Jim their current address, so he thought I would be in Miami.

Seeing the note "call Brownie" in Jim's notebook was like being elected president of the USA.

Al Brown next to Lt. Pringle. Near Salzburg, Austria, shortly after the end of WWII

I do not recall the other soldier's name. He was a lieutenant who joined us after Nurnburg.

My Two Cents

Al Brown 2008

Defenseless America

Prior to WWII, very few citizens realized how defenseless their country was. Well, prior to WWII, America was not able to stop an invasion from the tiny island of Japan on the far side of the Pacific Ocean!

After Pearl Harbor, the Third Infantry Division was spread out along the West Coast to stand off a feared invasion from Japan. The division's orders were that in the event of an amphibious attack, not to stop the invaders but to keep falling back and to fight only delaying actions. They were to buy as much time as possible while the country frantically mobilized its military. I know this because many of the soldiers who were in the division at that time were still with the division when I joined it in Italy. These soldiers told me about their orders during the invasion scare.

According to information I found via Google, shortly before the Japanese wiped out a large portion of our navy in a sneak attack at Pearl Harbor, our standing army numbered two hundred thirty thousand men. And a large number of them were lost as the Japanese swept over them in overwhelming numbers in the Philippines. Two years later, our army numbered eight million eight hundred thousand.

Would you suspect that before Pearl Harbor our army might have been just a mite understrength?

The numbers for our navy were no better, especially after Pearl Harbor. At that time there was no US Air Force. It was the Army Air Corps and was under Army Command.

Most of the US population was brainwashed into believing that, after we mobilized, we were the best-trained, best-equipped army in the world. Wrong! We were poorly equipped, short on training, and with zero combat experience.

Visualize if you will, an army of 230,000 becoming an army of 8,800,000 almost overnight, figuratively speaking. How were 8,800,000 to be trained by a mere 230,000 who did have some training? Only a very, very few of them had any battle experience. (There were a few who had fought in WWI.) How could you suddenly have 1,000,000 capable, trained, experienced officers to lead this new army? If you are going to get a grasp of the situation, you must ponder those things.

We were a bunch of civilians trying desperately to become competent soldiers. Most of our officers had no more military experience than the men they were leading. It was blind leading the blind. We all learned together *after* we were thrown into combat.

In the beginning, we were no match for the German Army. It was very disciplined, well trained, and equipped with the latest technology and weapons at the time and had several years of combat experience. By contrast, we began in North Africa in 1942 using WWI weapons and WWI tactics. Gradually our weapons got better, but never equal to Germany's, and as the war ground on, we learned to fight.

Because our country was so ill prepared, our casualties were easily double what they should have been.

Why do I bore you with all of this? I bore you because I am eighty-six years old, and my time to make a difference is very limited. Please, study history. Learn from it.

Glory

During my World War Two military service I was just like almost all of my comrades-in-arms. We were highly patriotic and naive to the extreme.

That is not to say that my patriotism made me want to be in the infantry. No sane person could possibly want to live under the most difficult and degrading conditions while taking part in human slaughter. No, I would have preferred any assignment other than the one I drew. My patriotism made it possible for me to accept the assignment. It was my firm belief then, as it is now, that every able bodied man has an obligation to protect and fight for the survival of the society in which he lives and benefits. While the infantry would never have been my choice, I accepted it as my lot. It was a nasty job and someone had to do it. Why should I be privileged and exempt?

But now, knowing what I have learned about the conduct of the war by a few of the high ranking generals and their incompetence and callous disregard for the lives of the men entrusted to their leadership, I have a totally different view of WWII.

There were the prima donnas: George S. Patton and Mark W. Clark to name two. They put childish rivalry for "glory" ahead of winning the war in as efficient a manner as possible.

One example is a Patton quote from "America's Forgotten Army", by Charles Whiting. In Sicily, wanting to get credit for taking Messina, General Patton gave the following order to General Bradley, Commander of II Corps, "I want you to get into Messina just as fast as you can. I don't want to waste time on these maneuvers even if you have to spend men to do it. I want to beat Monty into Messina."

Oh, I wish this was an isolated incident, but it was not. As I read historical accounts of WWII, I find this attitude quite prevalent among a few of our commanders.

Another example of "glory" ahead of winning was when General Mark Clark ordered General Truscott to abandon his battle plan to cut Highway 6 after the breakout from Anzio Beachhead. And, instead, turn 180 degrees and head for Rome, because he wanted his Fifth Army to beat the British Eighth Army to the Italian Capital.

Cutting Highway 6 was the prime objective that justified the Anzio invasion in the first place.

Had Clark allowed Truscott to carry out his plan, we would have had no trouble cutting Highway 6 and driving deeper into the rear of the German Army that was withdrawing from the Casino Front. The front opposing the Beachhead had collapsed and enemy resistance was light and sporadic. We would have trapped the bulk of Germany's army in Italy and forced its surrender.

As it turned out, this army escaped and survived to fight our soldiers in Italy to the end of the war. There is no way to calculate the increased loss of Allied Troops at the hands of these combat units after their escape from the Casino Front.

Also, the 20,000 plus casualties suffered by the Allies during the four-months of hell on Anzio Beachhead were pretty much wasted when the primary objective was tossed away in trade for some childish "glory".

If we Dogfaces had known then, what we know now, I doubt that we would have had the zeal and motivation to succeed. I know that I would have been reluctant to stick my neck out for some general's "glory".

Generals are frequently raving about the "Glory" on a battlefield. During my approximately 360 days of combat status, I have yet to see one incident of "Glory".

Disclaimer:

I want to be specific about a few generals who were NOT in the same category as the two generals mentioned above.

They were: Generals Omar Nelson Bradley, Alexander M. Patch, Lucian K. Truscott, John W. (Mike) O'Daniel, Troy H. Middleton, 45th Div., Charles W. Ryder, 34th Div., and Fred L. Walker, 36th Div. Of course there were many other good generals, but I want to make sure that these seven good generals, whose leadership impacted on me in one way or another, do not get placed in the wrong category.

My Enemy Was Not My Enemy

My enemy was the politicians who sent him. Someone before me said, "The soldiers win the wars and the politicians lose the peace." What a truth that is!

I did not hate the soldiers who opposed me. I had a great respect for them. The great majority were honorable, brave, well trained, and disciplined. They were good soldiers and fought doggedly, even against overwhelming odds.

The German soldier's foxhole was often no more than a hundred yards from mine. He had to put up with the same hardships as I did. His hole was not cozy and warm while mine was cold, wet, and miserable. Our jobs were the same. We just wore different uniforms. He was defending his country. I was defending mine.

Their politicians put them on a mission that could not succeed. During the last year of the war, the German soldier was overwhelmingly outnumbered in men, materials, and equipment. Yet he made us pay dearly for each and every victory. I had great respect for that even though I did not like it.

I write this because I have been told by my friend Albrecht, whom you have met if you have read my memoir

"Koppelschloss," that many German civilians had little respect for the German soldiers after the war because they were losers. I just want to set the record straight. They lost, but they were not losers.

The Niceties of War

As Roosevelt said, "I hate wah!" However, politicians of the world, ours included, make war a necessary evil. Therefore, I do support it when it is in the nation's best interest or for our survival.

We are constantly searching for more efficient and devious means of killing and maiming each other. World War II was no exception. Both sides were constantly finding new ways to kill and maim each other through mines and various devises dubbed "booby traps."

Early in the war the Germans learned that our jeeps, and a few other vehicles, had windshields that would fold down and that our drivers, in warm weather, would often drive with the windshield down. Taking advantage of this, the Germans began stretching piano wire across the streets and highways at just the right height to clear the hood. This was a very effective guillotine. To counter this, we welded an upright steel post on the front bumper. Near the top of this post was a notch or hook that would catch and break the wire.

The German schu-mine was insidious. It was a wooden box roughly 2"x4"x6" in size and was designed so that they could vary the explosive charge. A maximum charge would almost always kill the victim. A minimum charge would remove or seriously mangle a foot. It was buried just below the ground surface and was detonated whenever it was stepped on. They usually opted for the minimum charge. A wounded enemy was better than a dead one. A wounded soldier required other soldiers and facilities to care for him and was therefore more of a burden to our war effort. Being made of wood, it was almost undetectable by our mine detectors. These devices were used in great number and caused a great number of casualties, mostly to our riflemen who were almost always first to encounter them.

They had another insidious device that we dubbed "castrator." It was nothing more than a pistol barrel with a live round in the chamber. It was buried vertically with the end of the barrel at the ground surface. The cartridge's firing cap rested on a firing pin beneath it. When the barrel was stepped on, the cartridge fired. The bullet almost always struck the victim in the groin area and sometimes would enter the head via the chin area.

And then there was what we dubbed "the bouncing betty." It was a cylindrical canister containing explosive surrounded by ball bearings, nails, and/or small pieces of scrap metal. The trip wire triggered an explosive charge under the canister. When tripped, the canister was propelled upward, and the canister would then detonate when waist high, sending nails, ball bearings, and scrap metal in all directions. This device was especially vicious because it could kill or maim at much greater distance than a ground mine.

The Germans set all manner of traps for our mine clearing personnel. Quite often they would set a second mine below another mine so that after the top mine was neutralized and it was lifted, the lifting of the top mine detonated the bottom mine. Normally, mines with trip wires were set to detonate when more tension was applied. Occasionally, they would set them to detonate when tension was released. This caused our people to very carefully attach a string to the trip wire and move to a nearby hole or ditch to pull the string to detonate the mine. To counter that practice, the Germans would sometimes set dummy mines with trip wires and place a live one in the nearest hole or ditch. When the trip wire was pulled by the string, the real mine was detonated.

It was a constant one-upmanship game that both sides played. It was highly risky to touch anything that the Germans left behind. There was nothing that they would not use to their advantage. German pistols, cameras, wallets, and purses were prized souvenirs that our guys were trapped by. I was never a souvenir hunter. I touched nothing the enemy left behind. Read my memoir "Beer in Zweibrucken."

By their nature, booby traps are basically defensive weapons. By the time the US got into the war, Germany was mostly the defender and the Allies were the attackers. This gave Germany an almost exclusive advantage in the booby trap game. However, we also made extensive use of mines whenever we were in defensive positions. The stalemated positions on Anzio Beachhead and along the Casino Front are prime examples.

We dogfaces also improvised occasionally. One trick that was available to the dogface was the hand grenade. It was discovered that our fragmentation grenade would fit nicely in a C ration can, thus preventing the safety lever from releasing. Remove the can and the safety lever would fly off and the grenade would arm. We would place grenades twenty or thirty yards in front of our positions with a string tied to the can. We could then pull the string to remove the can from the grenade whenever an enemy was closing in. In five seconds the grenade exploded. In the mountains, where often patrol activity was limited to trails, our patrols would leave behind grenades in C ration cans for enemy patrols to kick over in the dark of night.

We humans are a strange lot. We have our Geneva Conferences to agree on civilized, gentlemanly rules for conducting wars, and then we are so ungentlemanly in the way we conduct them.

German Schu-mine 42 (Wikipedia)   German "S" mine a.k.a. Bouncing Betty (Wikipedia)

The Truth about the US WWII Bazooka

Early in the war, the US wanted an infantry weapon that could be used against enemy tanks. As a result, they developed a rocket-launched missile intended to penetrate armor. The explosive charge was cone shaped with the open end of the cone forward. Because of the shape, most of the explosive force was directed forward in a small circular pattern.

In my basic training, this weapon was demonstrated for us, and we were trained to fire it. The weapon was demonstrated by firing it at close range into a one-inch thick steel plate. When I examined the target, I was totally unimpressed. The only damage was a cone-shaped hole like the hole in a window pane that has been shot with an air rifle. The hole made by the rocket was less than an inch in diameter on the outside and barely an inch in diameter on the inside. I had my own opinion of its ability to penetrate the German tanks with armor several inches thick and made of much harder steel than the steel plate used in the demonstration.

My evaluation was borne out later in combat. It was soon discovered that the bazooka rocket would hardly faze German tanks. But it was discovered that a well-placed bazooka rocket would, occasionally, damage a track and make the tank immobile and vulnerable to attack with other weapons.

Now, when the Germans saw our rocket launcher, they decided that we had a good idea. So they developed one that would knock out our tanks. It was called Panzerschreck. Their rocket's cone shaped warhead was five inches (125mm) in diameter compared to our warhead that was 2.37 inches (60mm) in diameter. It is a mathematical fact that objects of the same shape will vary in volume as the cube of the relative dimensions. That volumetric difference gave the German rocket more than nine times the striking power of our rocket.

Comparing the cube of relative rocket dimensions: 2.37x2.37x2.37 = 13.31; and: 5x5x5 = 125

Therefore the power ratio between the two rockets was: 125/13.31 = 9.39/1

If the above is not convincing, try pure logic. If our rocket would penetrate their tanks, why would the Germans build a larger rocket to knock out our tanks that were easier to penetrate than their tanks? Why waste explosive power on overkill? It wasn't overkill, but it was enough to do the job. The German rocket knocked out far too many of our tanks.

Since all infantry weapons and equipment are carried by individual soldiers, it is important that each item be as light and as small as practical. Maneuverability is critical to infantry soldiers. Why, then, did the Germans build their Panzerschreck much larger and cumbersome than ours? They did it because it was necessary to make it effective. End of story!

Our bazooka did have its uses though. It was effective against lightly armored reconnaissance vehicles, trucks, passenger-type vehicles, machine gun positions, and things of that nature.

I have just read the citations of thirty-seven Medal of Honor recipients. Not one of them involves knocking out an enemy tank with a bazooka. Only one citation even involves the use of a bazooka. In that instance, S/Sgt. Clyde L. Choate, Company C, 601st Tank Destroyer Battalion, after his tank was knocked out, disabled a German medium tank by firing a bazooka rocket into one of its treads. After the tank was disabled, Staff Sergeant Choate shot the crew as they exited the tank.

If our bazooka would knock out German tanks, there would have been a lot of medals given for doing so. I have no firsthand knowledge of anyone knocking out a German tank with a bazooka. Damaged treads yes, but no penetration of the armor. On the other hand, there many times our rockets struck without damage.

After trumping us on the bazooka, Germany went a step further and came out with the Panzerfaust (iron fist). The Panzerfaust had a bazooka-type warhead but was launched from the end of a tube about two inches in diameter and maybe three feet long. They made the warhead in a variety of sizes, all of which would knock out any of our tanks. The Panzerfaust pretty much replaced their Panzerschreck, because the Panzerfaust was not nearly as cumbersome, and one man could easily carry six or more of them. They had a special canvaslike bag that they could be carried in.

I found it hard to believe that our country did not learn from this and give its infantry a weapon that did the job. Instead, they increased the diameter of our bazooka projectile from 2.37" to 3.5" (88mm). The 3.5" was also inadequate. Read my memoir "A Dash in the Snow." The leaders who provided such an inadequate weapon and taught our soldiers that it was lethal are responsible for that soldier's death and all the others who committed bazooka suicide.

Back to our previous math and physics lesson: 3.5X3.5x3.5 = 42.875; 125/42.875 = 2.92

So you see, the German rocket still had nearly three times the striking force as our 3.5".

The Germans didn't stop there. They made a large number of different sizes of the Panzerfaust. One was ten inches in diameter. 10 cubed equals one thousand. 1,000/42.875 = 23.32 times as powerful as our larger 3.5".

Following is a table showing Germany's overall production of their various infantry antitank weapons (this table was acquired from Google Web site):

Table 1: Overall Production

Production Figures	1943	1944	1945 (Jan, Feb, Mar)	Total
Faustpatrone	123,900	1,418,300	12,000	1,554,200
Panzerfaust 30, 60, 100, 150	227,800	4,120,500	2,351,800	6,700,100
Panzerschreck, RPzB.54 (-12/1944) and RPzB.54/1 (1945)	50,835	238,316	25,744	289,151
Panzerschreck ammunition (RPzB.Gr. 4322 and 4992)	173,000	1,805,400	240,000	2,218,400

Most notable is the huge amount of Panzerfausts produced. What makes these production figures even more impressive is the fact that nearly all of those were indeed issued to troops: in March 1945, the German forces possessed 3.018 million Panzerfausts, of which only 271,000 were stored in armories. The rest were distributed among the fighting forces. The overall production of the German Panzerfaust variants (Faustpatrone and Panzerfaust 30, 60, 100, and 150) is therefore 8,254,300.

Note that, according to the info above, these weapons were in the field where they were put to good use.

Their use was not limited to attacking our armor. They used them freely against our infantry. The Panzerfaust was especially useful in towns and villages. Where we liked to toss in a hand grenade prior to entering a room or building, they were able to place a Panzerfaust warhead in buildings from a much greater distance than with a hand grenade.

The Panzerfaust had another very significant advantage. The bazooka required the soldier to expose himself by kneeling or standing to fire it. The Panzerfaust could be fired from a prone, concealed position.

Our country could have easily provided us with such a weapon, but did not. This was a major failing.

by courtesy of M. Yrjola

Pup Tent Poets

No history of World War Two would be complete without mentioning "Pup Tent Poets". "Pup Tent Poets" was a regular feature in the overseas newspaper "Stars and Stripes Mediterranean". It was probably second only to Bill Mauldin's cartoons for entertainment and morale boosting.

Poems were accepted without consideration of rank or status. It provided a means of coping with the war and letting off steam.

I have included the "Foreword" and a few poems from a book publication of selected verses that had been in the "Stars and Stripes".

Foreword

Throughout the Mediterranean Theater of war, it is respectable to be a poet.
   Men in uniform who might once have regarded poetry as a matter for "long hairs" and "softies," are writing poems themselves and, what's more, signing them.
   Truck drivers are no less inclined toward the muse than the company cook; a machinegunner will dash off a verse during the lull of battle; the stony-faced topkick is producing love lyrics, and there's a laureate in every company. As one CO remarked:
   "It's a wonder we get any work done."
   The birth of the Puptent Poet took place more than two years ago when The Stars and Stripes, Mediterranean, in its first issue published in Algiers, opened its columns to soldier verse.
   It was a modest beginning. A mail censor named Lt. Gillespie turned in a few stanzas on the theme that he had accidentally slashed up one of his own letters while censoring company mail. The next issue contained a cynical, anonymous verse berating the thick mud of Oran.
   It may not have been apparent at the time, but the two versifiers had set a pattern for two years of Mediterranean poetry. From the beginning, the poetry department of The Stars and Stripes was open to all ranks. Furthermore, no one had to be a great poet, nor even a very good one to break into print.

Poems came in faster than the editors had dared to hope. From Casablanca to the sand-swept wadis of Tunisia, soldiers struck out boldly, discovering first that some things were better said in poetry than prose and, second, that The Stars and Stripes would publish what they wrote.

Critical standards set by newspapers in the United States were never adopted. Poetry critics were not allowed on the premises. What went into the paper was the best of the Army's verse-making that day, or that week. If the meter was wobbly and the rhymes eccentric or missing, no one got excited.

In two years of Puptent Poetry, no great war poet has revealed himself. What the Puptent Poets department has provided is a kind of open forum whose only requirements are a poetic leaning and an interest in writing about the war as well as living it. The result has been about 1,000 published poems in a little more than two years, and about 15 times that figure filed or returned to the writer with a note of regret.

Returning these notes and encouraging the Puptent Poets to try again has given Cpl. John Welsh, III, of Washington, D. C., a steady job as chief poetry editor and has made him one of the busiest correspondents in the theater.

Together with Cpl. Charles A. Hogan, of Trenton, N. J., who served as poetry editor of the Naples edition before going to France in a similar capacity, Cpl. Welsh compiled this the first Stars and Stripes Puptent Poet anthology.

—The Editors

HATRED'S YIELD

I've seen "the crosses row on row,"
I've seen the graves at Anzio
In Flanders fields men cannot sleep—
Their faith, the world found hard to keep.
Versailles' fate was slyly sealed
Before earth's gaping wounds had healed,
And now again rows of crosses
Mutely tell of nations' losses.
In how many fields,
In how many lands
Will soldiers die by soldiers' hands?
Until at long last mankind yields
To truth and reason's studied choice
Ignoring hatred's strident voice.
    —Pvt. Jack P. Nantell

HEY BUD

Hey Bud,
Watch out, will ya! This one's close!
Whoops! Whatta splash! That's a dud!
Where in the hell . . . ya goin'?

Hey Bud,
Stop, will ya? Ain'cha scared?
Looka that grass red with blood!
Why d'ya keep on goin'?
Ya don't wanna kill do ya?
But ya gonna kill, by God
Ya gotta get goin'.

Hey Bud,
Ya tired? Wanna go ta bed?
Don't go ta sleep in that mud!

—Oh—gotta a hole—in—ya—head
Sorry—Bud—
I'll—I'll keep on goin'.

—Sgt. Masque

ORDER

"At eight AM we're pulling out,"
The general sternly said,
So the colonel sent the order down,
"At five we leave our bed."
Well, the captain took no chances,
Because captains never do,
And so he told the topkick,
"Have the men get up at two."
At midnight the sergeant woke us,
And here we sadly sit,
Because it now is noontime,
And we haven't pulled out yet.
　　　　　—T-5 Carl D. Westerberg

DIRTY GERTIE[*1]

Dirty Gertie from Bizerte
Hid a mousetrap 'neath her skertie,
Strapped it on her kneecap purty,
Baited it with Fleur de Flirte,
Made her boy friends most alerty,
She was voted in Bizerte
"Miss Latrine" for nineteen-thirty.
     —Pvt. William L. Russell

---

[*] The original version of "Dirty Gertie," published in YANK, differed slightly from the verse reprinted in The Stars and Stripes. While "Gertie" was not a protege of "Puptent Poets," the editors felt nonetheless that she should be included in any collection of "the girls" discovered by Mediterranean military meanderers.

FANNY OF TRAPANI

Rumor has it "Dirty Gertie,"
Whom you knew in old Bizerte,
Has a sister in Trapani
By the name of Filthy Fanny.
She is Gertie's black-sheep sister,
No man yet has ever kissed her,
Though her friends have never told her
Awful is her body odor.
What a frightful-looking creature!
Badly formed in every feature!
When she ran for "MISS LATRINE"
The judges cried for Atabrine.
Fellows, now that you're in Trapani,
Be on the watch for "Filthy Fanny."
　　　　　　　—Cpl. F. D. Conner

LUSCIOUS LENA

Luscious Lena from Messina,
Cutest thing you've ever seena;
All the GI's dream—a queena!
Oh, that skin of sultry sheena!
When you go into Messina,
She will drink from your canteena;
She won't sock you on the beana,
But will purr like a machina.
When you walk through fields so greena.
With this lovely, luscious Lena;
She will say: "No go—bambina . . ."
(Hard to keep this ending cleena).
—Cpl. Fred Fischer
Pfc. Floyd Allchin

MARIE OF NAPOLI

My fair Marie of Napoli
Has taste and more
Her figure's round,
A perfect thirty-four.
Her build is slight,
Her step is light,
Her lips are sweet as dew.
Her cheek so fair, her silken hair,
Her eyes of gold-flecked brown;
The merest touch, and you want to clutch
The neatest stuff in town.
But halt your glim, for your chance is slim,
Forget your dearest wish,
It's tough stuff, lad, and just too bad
But you see, I found her first!
—Pvt. James F. Dunne

ANZIO

A flare-lit night, a frosty breeze
The chequered light of moon through trees
The gelid, quiv'ring battle glow
This is Nero's Anzio.

The monster stalks; his cannon roar
Is this Dunkirk, Corregidor?
In sharp riposte our guns bark "No"
"These are the men of Anzio."

By day the wedgewood sky is bright
With vapor trails of Allied might;
By night the scudding clouds resound
With sounds of war from air and ground.

Against this mighty fist of nail
Our lines hold firm,
They shall not fail,
Thus slowly, Europe's bloodstained yoke
Is seized from puerile herrenvolk.

This inchoate beach, this spot of sand
Beyond the Paperhanger's hand
Will share in history's hallowed glow
Remember it, this Anzio.
 —Lt. Richard Oulahan Jr.

AIR RAID

The searchlights probe the startled night
And pin the bombers like string-held kites,
On beamed untwinkling stars of white.
The AA guns shout parrying fight,
And defy in a chorus of stammering might;
Their darting fingers are seeking bright
A pattern of deadly streaks of spite.
The bombs strike down, far left, far right
And mushrooming rumbled blights
Of noise respond . . . a hit ignites
And the fire tongues up to dizzy heights,
A broken bomber falls in tight
Plunging arcs, out, out of sight;
Then suddenly baffled, unrequite,
The planes wheel off in shaken flight—
The "all-clear" siren shrilling writes
An end to the hell of sound and light.
—Lt. John T. Weaver

I HUNT TODAY

In bygone days, I used to hunt
The swiftly flying duck
And stalk through woods of birch and pine
To bag an eight-point buck.
I used to seek to flush the quail
That plump and wary fowl
And oft at night my roaring gun
Would end the coyote's howl.
I've faced the charged wounded moose,
I've felt the jaguar's claws,
I've faced the tiger's snarling growl,
The lion's hungry roars,
I've looked into the jaws of death,
And never had to pray,
But God, please give me courage,
I'm hunting "man" today.
—St. A. Schneider

THE RANGERS *2

Cool breath of evening
Softly gowned in velvet,
Diademed—
Hail Mary Full Of Grace;
Our Father Who Art In . . .
"Fall In!"
The jump-off:
"Ready. READY! here we go . . ."
Wonder if this time . . .

South of Rome, the beachhead:
Infiltrate, CISTERNA—cut the Appian way!
Tomorrow the day; tonight,
We march . . .
Veterans, battle-tried and steady
Rough hewn, weaponed, ready.
Rifles, bazookas, sticky grenades, bandoleers.
Rangers and Destiny nears—
Lead on soldiers here we go,
Through the ditches to Cisterna, traveling light,
March through the night,
Ghosts of Clark and Indian Rangers

Rogers and his rugged Rangers
Stalk the dark. They walk
Beside you, fellow Rangers—
Plod along easy . . . Quiet!

The silent night, cloud cloaked skies
Hide the danger that lies ahead.
The early dawn peers, stares
Where stalk the Rangers . . . Beware!
Here in strength the enemy lies
Poised for the kill.
But life as the rolling tide at will
Moves on. So the Rangers.

Near the edge of town
Flame stabbed, rock-walled, houses awake,
Mortars, artillery, tanks-blast and shake
To tear open the ranks of the Rangers.
Sunrise spells doom:
The dawn is now for the Rangers!
The Flight is on.

Men against tanks
Which line the road and banks;
Churn the fields; blast the woods
And the ditches! . . . Charge the tanks!
Rifles and blades, and sticky grenades.
Blast the treads: hurl yourself against tanks!
Ere your ranks are all gone
Barehanded men fight on.

Oh bloodied fields, ditches, woods,
Bloodied Rangers!

To the dangers of death you're not strangers.
Free men can die, must die
Till the danger that stalks
The Ranger is past.
Hark to the ghosts of Rogers and Clark:
Hark to the Rangers!
To the tomahawks that stalk
Until peace talks, and Freedom's light
Once more is bright
Over all the land.

They, too, marched through the dangers;
March on with THE RANGERS.

—F. Riley

---

* On January 30, 1944, two battalions of Rangers spearheaded an attack on Cisterna from the Anzio beachhead, then one week old. They were surrounded and cut off by the Germans Only a handful escaped. The rest were killed or captured.

CONVERSATION WITH A MULE

Now, Mule, you say you work too hard,
That you have a life of pain,
You never seem to get a rest
Through ice and sleet or rain.
You climb the highest mountains,
But remember I do, too.
You have four legs to take you home,
But me—I've only two.
And when our journey's over
And the time has come to eat,
A generous hand brings food to you
While you rest your weary feet.
I carry mine for miles and miles,
Have C rations every day,
Unless my luck's against me
And the cook throws me a "K."
And when it's time for us to sleep
There's one thing I can say,
I have to sleep on mountain tops
While you bed down on hay.
Now, Mule, would you take my place,
Even though you know you couldn't?

Would you be content with a life like mine?
You know darn well you wouldn't!
—Pvt. Richard Hiorns

THE MULE REPLIES

Dear Dick, you wrote and asked me,
If I'd trade my place with you
Because you think my life is free
And I've little work to do.
Well, brother, for your information
I work like hell to the very last,
And no matter what the situation
I still end up a sad, old ass.
Look at me in this same old hide,
Wouldst thou wear this ugly skin?
Would you daily drink from riversides
And forsake your whiskey and your gin?
And I can't get a small promotion
No matter if I work both hard and fast,
But you at the very slightest notion
Rise up to rank of private—yes—first class.
Now, Dick, after all I've told you,
If you still wanna be a mule,
Your request will not be considered,
For we won't accept so big a fool.
—Lt. Bernard Knighten

Photo Gallery

Third Division photographers Bill "Pop" Heller, Bobby Seesock, Bill Toomey, John Cole and Howard Nickelson (l-r) spend Christmas 1944, in decent surroundings in Ribeauville, Colmar Pocket. (courtesy dogfacesoldiers.org)

Jebsheim was one of a string of fortified towns in the north to south communication grid east of Colmar. The 254th Regiment, newly attached to the Third Division, was tested in its first combat in the Colmar Pocket. The Regiment cleared 1,000 prisoners in three days of fierce fighting at Jebsheim. (courtesy dogfacesoldiers.org)

General DeGaulle ordered the pomp and circumstance for a February 20 ceremony in Colmar awarding the American Third Division the Croix de Guerre with Palm for its action in the Colmar Pocket. A second Croix de Guerre for its action in the Vosges campaign allowed the Third Division to wear the French Fourragere. (courtesy of dogfacesolsdiers.org)

Crowning their Ribeauville tree, Third Division photographers pass Christmas 1944 facing the German army still entrenched in the Colmar Pocket. To the north the Battle of the Bulge was at a critical point, and to come was the German Nordwind offensive of Dec. 31-Jan. 25 that would threaten the Seventh Army and VI Corps in the south. (courtesy dogfacesoldiers.org)

General de Lattre de Tassigny decorates Third Division Commander Gen. John O'Daniel with the Legion d'Honneur, third degree and the Croix de Guerre with Palm for leading his division in the Colmar Pocket at Feb. 20 ceremonies in Colmar. The Third Division was also awarded a Presidential Unit Citation for the same action, the first and one of only four awarded to a full division during the war. (courtesy dogfacesoldiers.org)

PFC Steven R. Lakos of the Third Division contemplates the enemy in death at Ostheim, France during action in the Colmar Pocket January 1945. So overshadowed by the news of the Battle of the Bulge, the equally-heroic Allied action around Colmar and Strasbourg became known as the "forgotten war." (courtesy dogface soldiers.org)

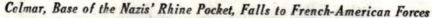

The Stars and Stripes issued February 4, 1945 announced the end of the German's occupation of the Colmar Pocket. (courtesy dogfacesoldiers.org)

A Grave Registration unit operates ten miles north of Colmar in Ribeauville bringing war down to the numbers. By the time the Colmar action was through, the Third Division would mark 4,500 casualties since it's southern France landing. (courtesy dogfacesoldiers.org)

After assembly at Carpentras, the Third Division's 15th Regiment moved northwest at 0500 on August 26 to join the fight. Forward units approached Montelimar along Highway 7 and met resistance on August 27. (courtesy dogfacesoldiers.org)

Photographer Bill Toomey reflects over a letter to home from Strasbourg, France in mid-December 1944. The war would not be over by Christmas as the commanders in the north had hoped and the Allied armies had not yet felt the sting of the last German offensive attacks of the war.

(Author's comment: Bill Toomey, as part of the 3rd Reconnaissance Platoon, was one of the photographers who took the photos appearing in the dogfacesoldiers.org web site. Bill's son, Denis Toomey, is the web master and it is with Denis' generous permission that the dogfacesoldiers.org images are reprinted in this book.) (courtesy dogfacesoldiers.org)

Photographer's Jack Cole and Bill Heller pose with the tools of their trade on a warm September day in Faucogney, France. Jack and Bill were part of 3rd Division Recon Platoon that provided most of the images appearing on the website dogfacesoldiers.org. (courtesy dogfacesoldiers.org)

General Patch honors an unidentified soldier in Epinal, France. Epinal is the sight of a 48-acre memorial cemetery with 5,250 American dead including four Medal of Honor recipients. (courtesy dogfacesoldiers.org)

The drive north from Lure to Faucogney was fiercely contested—the fighting at times hand to hand. The retreat of the German army was slowed as it fell back into prepared positions and advancing Americans faced booby-traps in ordinary things. The advance also encountered massive wooden roadblocks manned more and more by fanatical defenders. (courtesy dogfacesoldiers.org)

Dogies on 601st Tank Battalion tank. Beats walking. (courtesy dogfacesoldiers.org)

As the Third took position, 15th Regiment troops advanced into violent combat and incessant counterattacks. The 7th Regiment entered Montelimar from the southeast on the 29th where three battalions of the 7th and 30th regiments crossed a small river to the east of the town during the morning as they continued to attack. (courtesy dogfacesoldiers.org)

All three of the Third Division's regiments were active in the attack on Montelimar as they joined the 36th Division in seizing the town. German strength approached three divisions strong with the veteran 11th Panzer Division as the pivot. (courtesy dogfacesoldiers.org)

German prisoners, including wounded soldiers wait for final processing on Red Beach. In the first 24 hours, Third Division units captured more than 1,500 soldiers mostly from the 242nd Infantry Division which was later destroyed in its defense of Toulon. At the hands of the Third Division, the Germans suffered 330 killed, 1,005 wounded and 9,000 captured in the days surrounding the landings. (courtesy dogfacesoldiers.org)

The nine-day battle at Montelimar cost the German army dearly in the midst of unimaginable horror. The final convoy leaving Montelimar on August 29, with 2,000 vehicles of all type including horse-drawn transportation, was trapped on a 14 kilometer stretch of Highway 7 to the north. Deadly artillery fire and a few fighter bomber attacks claimed a grim reward. (courtesy dogfacesoldiers.org)

Al & other Co. H friends Salzburg May 1945

Al with some of the men from his machinegun section
Salzburg, Austria, May 1945

Austria, May 1945
Company H, 30th Infantry ready for inspection

(The nearest two machineguns belong to 1st Section, 1st Platoon, Al's Section.)

Petitejeans re-visited in 2002

Second visit as farm hands July, 2002. Dinner at Laroches'.
(L-R, Philippe, Arlette, Virginie, Al & Michel)

Dinner at Laroches', July, 2002, with Roland Laroche on
camera duty.
(L-R Family friend, Jo Ann, Nathalie, Monique,
Philippe, Virginie, Michel)

2002—Jo feeding the lovely pampered ladies.

Dinner at Laroches', 2002, Roland pours the wine.

Friendly game before Nurenburg. The man to the left was a second Lieutenant newly arrived from the US. I wish that I could recall his name. Good officer, learned fast. That is me with the rifle. I always kept my rifle with me. You never knew when the enemy would surprise you, even in the most "secure" settings.

Lt. Jim Pringle among the rocks in the Vosges Mountains
(Al, you are somewhere in this rock pile, Jim.)

S/Sgt Albert S. Brown shortly after returning home from the war.

I shared more foxholes with Sgt. Chester F. Borowski than any other soldier. When we were on the move, he was almost always one position behind me. Chester was over six feet tall. I was five feet four inches. Whenever we encountered a ditch too wide, a rock or embankment too high, for me to negotiate, Chester would just take me by my pack harness and literally lift across or over the impediment.

Three Sons Overseas

Three sons of Mr. and Mrs. Wm. L. Brown are now in active service overseas. Ensign Beverly M. Brown has been on patrol and convoy duty aboard a subchaser since June 1943. He is now second in command and administrative officer of his ship somewhere in the Pacific. Private First Class Frank H. Brown and Private Albert S. Brown are in North Africa.

Anzio A Liability

Failure Of Latest Cassino Offensive Explained

By WES GALLAGHER

LONDON, March 29—(AP)—With military authorities conceding the failure of the latest Cassino offensive, the Anzio beachhead is regarded as virtually a liability under present conditions.

Nevertheless the situation in Italy was regarded today as looking more serious than it really is—because it is the only active land front held by the British and Americans in Europe. As other larger operations develop, it is expected the Italian campaign will fall into its proper perspective and thus give a clear picture why its operations have been limited.

The ground situation in Italy is secure but extremely difficult from a military viewpoint.

At the Anzio beachhead the Germans are fighting over internal lines of communication. In a single night they can move a division facing the beachhead south to face the main Fifth Army at Cassino, to beat off an attack there. Two nights later they can move it back if necessary to meet any beachhead thrust.

* * *

Conversely the Allies must move troops from the beachhead to the Fifth Army or in reverse, by the slow sea route. It would be extraordinary if a division could be moved from one of these fighting forces to another in a week.

Clearing weather, however, may give the air forces a chance to batter a hole in the German defenses just as they did in April and May last year in Tunisia.

The terrific bombing given Cassino fell short of expectations in two respects. In the first place a considerable number of Germans hidden in caves and tunnels escaped the bombing, came out of their hiding places after waves of infantry had passed and cut their lines of communication.

Secondly, tanks moving up behind the Allied infantry found they had to stay on only two roads available because the condition of the ground on either side was too bad to allow other movement. Bombs cratered the roads badly and these craters immediately filled with water, making it necessary for engineers to fill in each crater before tanks and trucks could move.

By this time the advanced infantry had to be supplied by air and the Germans were so well established they were able to block the advancing tanks, forcing the infantry to fight its way back.

While these were the causes for the immediate setback at Cassino, the fundamental reason for the slow progress is the same as it has been since the original Anzio landing failed to cause a German withdrawal on the Cassino front.

* * *

By nature, the Allied overall battle plan for the coming campaign in Western Europe, now in the full tide of preparation committed Italy to limited operations.

Progress could be made in Italy by throwing in countless thousands of Allied troops and disregarding losses, but the British-American combined staff decided the gains would not be worth the cost.

This leaves the field commanders in Italy the task of doing the job with the forces at hand. It had been hoped definite Allied air superiority would be enough to tip the scale of battle in the Fifth Army's favor because the ground forces are about equal. But bad weather kept the bombers from exerting their full power.

Even the volcano Vesuvius took a hand in the picture—showering hot rocks on the surrounding area and forcing the abandonment of at least two key air fields because of damage to planes.

HEADQUARTERS THIRTIETH INFANTRY
APO # 3   U.S. ARMY

31 May 1945

SUBJECT: Announcement of Award of Bronze Star.

TO : S/Sgt. Albert S. Brown, Company "H", 30th Infantry, APO # 3

1. You have been awarded the Bronze Star.

2. As your regimental commander, I congratulate you on your excellent service, both to your regiment and your country. It is the fine work of men like you that keep the 30th Infantry on top and make the United States Army the great fighting organisation that it is.

3. You will receive your ribbon at an appropriate ceremony in the near future.

LIONEL C. McGARR
Colonel, 30th Infantry,
Commanding.

Edwards Brothers, Inc.
Thorofare, NJ USA
October 27, 2011